POCKET GUIDE

TREES

OF SOUTHERN AFRICA

PIET VAN WYK

Revised & updated by
Braam van Wyk

Published by Struik Nature
(an imprint of Penguin Random House South Africa (Pty) Ltd)
Reg. No. 1953/000441/07
The Estuaries No. 4, Oxbow Crescent
Century Avenue, Century City, 7441
PO Box 1144, Cape Town, 8000 South Africa

Visit **www.penguinrandomhouse.co.za** and join the Struik Nature Club
for updates, news, events and special offers

First published 1993 as *A Photographic Guide
to Trees of Southern Africa*
Second edition 2001
Third reworked edition (*Pocket Guide:
Trees of Southern Africa*) 2013

5 7 9 10 8 6

Copyright © in text, 1993, 2001, 2013: Estate of P. van Wyk
Copyright © in photographs, 1993, 2001, 2013: Estate of P. van Wyk,
except where otherwise indicated
Copyright © in maps, 1993, 2001, 2013: Braam van Wyk
& Meg Coates Palgrave
Copyright © in published edition, 1993, 2001, 2013:
Penguin Random House South Africa (Pty) Ltd

Publisher: Pippa Parker
Managing editor: Helen de Villiers
Editors: Lisa Delaney, Colette Alves
Design director: Janice Evans
Designer: Gillian Black
Proofreader: Emsie du Plessis

Reproduction by Hirt & Carter Cape (Pty) Ltd
Printed and bound in China by Toppan Leefung Packaging and Printing
(Dongguan) Co., Ltd

ISBN 978 1 92057 202 0 (Print)
ISBN 978 1 77584 074 9 (ePUB)

Front cover: Quivertree – Gerhardt Dreyer/IOA
Back cover, top to bottom: Mountain hardpear – Braam van Wyk;
Matumi, Flametree, Wild-almond – Piet van Wyk
Title page: Umbrella thorn – Piet van Wyk
Opposite: Large copalwood – Piet van Wyk

Contents

Acknowledgements to the first edition

Anybody with some experience in field studies will appreciate that the cost of compiling a publication of this nature is enormous, since it entails extensive travelling and the consumption of vast quantities of film. Without the very generous assistance, therefore, of the companies, institutions and persons mentioned below, this book would never have been possible. I salute them all, since they deserve the deepest gratitude from not only myself but also the eventual users of this book and of other related publications currently in preparation.

Companies and institutions
- Mazda Wildlife Fund has placed a Mazda B2200 bakkie, with canopy, at my disposal.
- Agfa SA (Pty) Ltd supplies and develops all my film.
- Total SA (Pty) Ltd keeps the bakkie's fuel tank filled.
- APBCO (Insurance brokers, Pretoria) covers the insurance of the Mazda bakkie.
- Pick 'n Pay Stores Ltd.
- The University of Pretoria and the Rand Afrikaans University, whose departments of botany assist me academically, financially and administratively.

Individuals
Official
Agfa SA: Ron Crane, Marthinus Bezuidenhout, Barbara Garner; APBCO Brokers: Kobus du Plessis; Mazda Wildlife Fund: Peter Frost; Pick 'n Pay Stores: Brenda van der Schijff; Rand Afrikaans University: Ben-Erik van Wyk; Total SA: Andries van der Walt; University of Pretoria: Braam van Wyk, Elsa van Wyk, Martie Dednam.

Private
All are friends – some new, some of long-standing – who have helped me and my wife Emmarentia by providing accommodation, hospitality, access to national parks, nature reserves and botanical gardens, or rendered highly valued assistance with fieldwork: Jonathan Gibson (Chobe Lodge, Botswana); Chris Burgers, Neil and Thea Fairall (CPA Nature Conservation); Wayne Matthews, Nick Steele, Harold and Marieta Thornhill (KwaZulu Bureau for Natural Resources); Lloyd and June Wilmot and staff (Lloyd's Camp, Botswana); Roelf van Wyk (my brother); Daan Botha, Kobus Eloff and Dawie Strydom (National Botanical Gardens); Robbie Robinson (National Parks Board); Harold and Tony Braack (Richtersveld National Park); Veronica Roodt (student, Botswana); Niek Hanekom, Andrew Spies (Tsitsikamma Coastal National Park); Sarel Yssel (West Coast National Park).

Piet van Wyk
1993

Introduction

Interest in trees has been greatly boosted by 'green' awareness campaigns currently being conducted around the world. Not too long ago, scientists who sounded warnings about global warming (the greenhouse effect), ozone depletion, the unacceptable rate at which rain forests are being cleared, acid rain and so on, were either ignored or passed off as alarmists. Today, the seriousness of pollution and its destructive effects on our environment are widely acknowledged, prompting people to engage in positive action so as to avert an impending catastrophe. One of the first steps we can take is to familiarize ourselves with an area of concern and then become thoroughly acquainted with the remedy – and the ways in which it should be administered.

The purpose of this book is to 'whet the appetite' of the uninitiated and to encourage a desire among readers to become more knowledgeable about trees – particularly those of southern Africa – and their critical role in the environment.

The vegetation of southern Africa

Six so-called floristic kingdoms are recognized in the world. Two of them occur in southern Africa: the Cape Fynbos Kingdom, which roughly covers the winter-rainfall area of the Western Cape; and the Palaeotropic Kingdom, which covers nearly all of Africa. Seven well-marked, broadly defined vegetation zones (or

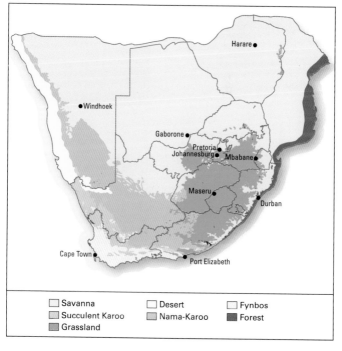

☐ Savanna	☐ Desert	☐ Fynbos
☐ Succulent Karoo	☐ Nama-Karoo	■ Forest
■ Grassland		

biomes) can be distinguished in southern Africa. Based on plant life forms and climate, they are: savanna (bushveld), forest, desert, succulent Karoo, Nama-Karoo, grassland and fynbos.

The largest of these areas, the **savanna** biome (also referred to as bushveld or woodland, including thicket) extends northwards from the Eastern Cape to cover parts of KwaZulu-Natal and Swaziland; most of Mpumalanga, Limpopo and the North West province; the Northern Cape, the northwestern Free State, Mozambique, Zimbabwe, Botswana, and northern and central Namibia. This region harbours most of the tree species on the subcontinent.

By far the smallest biome, **forest**, occurs intermittently and sometimes in only extremely small patches along the eastern escarpment in South Africa, from the eastern parts of the Western Cape to the Soutpansberg in Limpopo. Several hundred kilometres further north, forest reappears in the eastern, mountainous area of Zimbabwe and the western area of Mozambique.

The **desert** biome mainly corresponds with the Namib Desert in Namibia and extends in a relatively wide belt along the coast, northwards from Lüderitz. Tree species that are able to tolerate the harsh environmental conditions of this region are very limited.

Immediately south of the desert biome (and in a similar belt to the west of the western escarpment), the **succulent Karoo** biome can be found extending southwards into South Africa, at first along the coast and then on the inland side of the fynbos biome to the Little Karoo. Tree species are more numerous in this biome but still limited; they include some succulents, such as species of *Aloe*.

Although insignificant in extent, the **fynbos** biome is, floristically, extremely rich and complex. The number of tree species in this biome is fairly limited; however, most tree species here are unique.

The **Nama-Karoo** biome encompasses the central plateau of the Northern Cape, north of the southern mountain ranges. It extends east-west, including Lesotho, the southwestern Free State, the southern interior of Namibia and smaller parts in the Eastern Cape. As can be expected, only tree species that are drought-resistant and frost-tolerant can survive in this biome, which therefore excludes the bulk of those on the subcontinent.

Despite higher rainfall, very low winter temperatures in the **grassland** biome have resulted in much the same situation as in the Nama-Karoo. This area is wedged between the savanna biome on the southern, eastern, northern and northwestern sides and the Nama-Karoo biome on the southwestern side, therefore covering large parts of Mpumalanga, Gauteng, the North West province, most of the Free State, Lesotho, western KwaZulu-Natal and sections of the Eastern Cape.

Most tree species are limited to two biomes, namely forest and savanna. This is because the majority of plant species currently growing on the subcontinent started migrating southwards from Africa's tropical region at the end of the last Ice Age. They were adapted to high temperatures, especially during winter, and favourable moisture conditions during summer, both of which are characteristic of the biomes involved.

Within each of the biomes, conspicuous differences occur in the composition, structure and density of plant communities. These variations are attributable to the influence of moisture in an area, as well as differences in altitude, slope of the terrain, soil type and the prevalence of veld fires. In this regard, soil is one of the major factors, which is why the text frequently draws attention to the soil preferences of the different species.

For obvious reasons, a small proportion of southern Africa's approximate 2 100 tree species are included in this guide. Trees selected for inclusion are either widespread, attractive, representative of an outstanding group of related species, an important component within a specific biome, a valuable source of wood or other plant material, have outstanding potential as a garden subject, or are simply impressive.

When encountering a tree with which you are not familiar, establish whether it is dealt with in the book by comparing its leaves, flowers and/or fruit with the photographs, making sure that the distribution indicated on the map coincides with your own geographic location. Read through the text and then look at the photographs again. Whether you have correctly identified your tree or not, hopefully your interest (or frustration) will at this stage have been sufficiently aroused to make you hasten to the nearest bookshop to buy a more comprehensive book.

> **NOTE:** Common names of tree species are followed by FSA (national tree) numbers in parentheses. Namibian and Zimbabwean common names (and national tree numbers) are also supplied where relevant.

Further reading and references

Boon, R. 2010. *Pooley's Trees of Eastern South Africa,* 2nd edition. Flora and Fauna Publications Trust, Durban.

Coates Palgrave, M. 2005. *Keith Coates Palgrave Trees of Southern Africa,* 3rd edition, 2nd impression. Struik Publishers, Cape Town.

Funston, M. 1994. *Bushveld Trees, Lifeblood of the Transvaal Lowveld* (text by Borchert, P. & Van Wyk, B.). Fernwood Press, Vlaeberg.

Mannheimer, C. & Curtis, B. (eds) 2009. *Le Roux and Müller's Field Guide to the Trees and Shrubs of Namibia.* Macmillan Education Namibia, Windhoek.

Moll, E. 2011. *What's That Tree?* Struik Nature, Cape Town.

Palmer, E. & Pitman, N. 1972 & 1973. *Trees of Southern Africa.* 3 Vols. A.A. Balkema, Cape Town.

Schmidt, E., Lötter, M. & McCleland, W. 2007. *Trees and Shrubs of Mpumalanga and Kruger National Park,* 2nd edition. Jacana Media, Johannesburg.

Van Wyk, B., Van den Berg, E., Coates Palgrave, M. & Jordaan, M. 2011. *Dictionary of Names for Southern African Trees.* Briza Publications, Pretoria.

Van Wyk, B. & Van Wyk, P. 2007. *How to Identify Trees in Southern Africa.* Struik Publishers, Cape Town.

Van Wyk, B. & Van Wyk, P. 2013. *Field Guide to Trees of Southern Africa.* Struik Publishers, Cape Town.

Van Wyk, B., Van Wyk, P. & Van Wyk, B-E. 2008. *Photo Guide to Trees of Southern Africa,* 2nd edition. Briza Publications, Pretoria.

Van Wyk, P. 1972 & 1974. *Trees of the Kruger National Park,* 2 vols. Purnell, Johannesburg.

Van Wyk, P. 2008. *Field Guide to the Trees of the Kruger National Park,* 5th edition. Struik Publishers, Cape Town.

Journals

Journal of Dendrology. Dendrological Society. Pretoria.
Information contained within articles in this journal, written by various authors (mainly Fried and Jutta von Breitenbach), was freely used during the compilation of this publication.

Male cones

Seed

Outeniqua yellowwood (FSA16)

Podocarpus falcatus

Outeniekwageelhout

Distribution & habitat This species occurs in the forests of the far eastern corner of the Western Cape and to the east and west of Knysna (the Mecca of yellowwood furniture in South Africa). It is also found in all evergreen forests along the escarpment up to Limpopo, extending into Zimbabwe, Mozambique and the tropical areas to the north.

Description The trunk of the Outeniqua yellowwood can be up to 3 m in diameter and is always long and straight; it is sometimes slightly fluted. The dark brown bark peels off in large strips. At 45–50 m in height, the yellowwoods (especially *P. falcatus*) are among the tallest native trees in southern Africa. Tourists visiting the eastern parts of the Western Cape and travelling on the famous Garden Route cannot fail to notice this species, as the crowns of old trees tower above the forest canopy. Identification is further facilitated by the fact that most of them are 'decorated' with light grey lichen (old man's beard), which hangs from the branches in long strings. **LEAVES** Simple, straight or slightly falcate (sickle-shaped); they are the smallest of the four yellowwood species (up to 50 × 5 mm). **FRUITS** Round berries, which turn yellow when ripe; borne only on female trees.

Notes: This species, along with its relative, *P. latifolius*, is used for making furniture.

8

Male cones

Female cones

Mountain cypress (FSA20)

Widdringtonia nodiflora

Bergsipres

Distribution & habitat This tree grows on the escarpment mountains from Cape Town to the KwaZulu-Natal midlands, the Drakensberg of Mpumalanga and the Soutpansberg, as well as areas in the Waterberg region of Limpopo. It also extends into eastern Zimbabwe and Mozambique.

Description An evergreen with a single trunk and a spreading, fairly dense crown, it usually attains a height of about 6 m. The bark on old stems is grey and flakes in long, narrow strips, revealing the reddish brown living bark. **LEAVES** Needle-like when young; scale-like, minute and dark green when old. **CONES** Roughly round, up to about 25 mm in diameter, dark brown, with conspicuous protuberances. Male and female cones are borne on separate trees. Male cones are very small and borne on thin side-shoots (August–September), while female cones are borne on fairly thick stalks near branch-ends. They are persistent: cones in various stages of development may be found throughout the year.

(ZIMBABWE: (Z9) MOUNTAIN CEDAR)

Fruit

Lala palm (FSA23)   *Hyphaene coriacea*

Lalapalm

Distribution & habitat The two *Hyphaene* species of palm are distinctly separated, geographically. *H. coriacea* (previously *H. crinita* and *H. natalensis*) occurs along the coasts of the Eastern Cape, KwaZulu-Natal and Mozambique, inland in Mozambique and in the extreme south of the Mpumalanga lowveld. *H. petersiana* (previously *H. benguellensis*) grows in the northern areas of Namibia, Botswana, Zimbabwe, Limpopo and most of the Mpumalanga lowveld. Palm trees found in the northern and central parts of the Kruger National Park are now considered to be *H. petersiana*.

Description The most conspicuous difference between the two species is the shape of the fruit: *H. coriacea* has pear-shaped fruit, while *H. petersiana* has round fruit. **LEAVES** Large and fan-shaped; the petiole has sharp, hooked thorns. **FLOWERS** Small reproductive organs are borne within large flowers; each sex is on a separate tree. Male flowers are small, yellow-green and packed in longitudinal or spiral rows. Female flowers consist of small, green, spherical knobs, also arranged in rows. Flowering takes place in November–December. **FRUITS** Borne in large pendent clusters, they are dark brown, relatively large (60 mm in diameter), shiny and very hard when ripe; they reach maturity after approximately two years.

Notes: Sap collected from stems is used to brew an alcoholic beverage. In the process, stems are cut off and, although some may sprout again, others eventually die. This is one reason why full-grown trees are somewhat rare.

GERHARD DREYER/DA

Flowers

Quivertree (FSA29)

Kokerboom

Aloe dichotoma

Distribution & habitat Members of the *Aloe* genus are found mainly in Africa, the Arabian Peninsula and Madagascar. On the eastern side of the subcontinent, *A. barberae* is the more widespread, while on the arid western side, it is *A. dichotoma*. The quivertree has a relatively restricted distribution in the Northern Cape and adjoining Namibia to a point north of Windhoek. It is protected in several national parks in both countries.

Description All *Aloe* species have characteristic succulent leaves and, although quite a number have been incorporated in the national tree lists, only a few are truly tree-like (with a main trunk, conspicuous branches and a crown). In full-grown trees, the trunk is massive, measuring about 3 m in circumference at ground level, but tapering rapidly further up; it branches profusely. Branches are grey and smooth. The dark yellow bark flakes off in patches, causing the trunk to appear mottled. **LEAVES** Fairly small and situated only at branch tips; the crown is relatively dense. **FLOWERS** Pale yellow and borne on short spikes in branched, axillary inflorescences (June–July). Insects, birds and primates are attracted to the nectar. **FRUITS** Roughly oval with six distinct, longitudinal grooves; they resemble that of other *Aloe* species.

Notes: Simon van der Stel was the first to record this species, in 1685. The common name, quivertree, derives from the fact that San hunters fashioned quivers for their arrows from the soft branches. The wood itself is fibrous and useless.

Dehisced fruit with seeds   Crown

Flowers

Coastal strelitzia (FSA34)   *Strelitzia nicolai*

Kuswildepiesang

Distribution & habitat The coastal strelitzia, also known as the coastal wild banana, has the widest distribution of all the *Strelitzia* species in southern Africa, extending all along the coast from East London to southern Mozambique. Two other *Strelitzia* species occur in southern Africa: *S. alba*, which has a limited distribution in the coastal region of the far eastern parts of the Western Cape (Knysna) and *S. caudata*, which is associated with forests on the escarpment in Swaziland, Mpumalanga and Limpopo, reappearing again in the Chipinge/Mutare region of Zimbabwe and adjoining parts of Mozambique.
Description The three species are very similar and difficult to separate vegetatively. *S. nicolai* may reach about 8 m in height and, due to suckering, grows in large clumps.
LEAVES Banana-like with long, fairly stiff petioles and blades that are approximately 2 m long × 0.5 m wide. **FLOWERS** Borne in bluish, boat-shaped spathes, each consisting of three white, upright sepals and three petals (two are bright blue and lie close together, forming a structure that resembles an arrow-head; the third is small and frilled). Unlike in the two other species, these flowers are layered, multiple structures consisting of up to five spathes – each new one arising from the previous one. A slimy mucilage is produced within the spathe. **FRUITS** Three-lobed, woody capsules; each black seed is capped with a frilly, bright orange aril.

Notes: This is a beautiful garden subject that is widely used in the subtropical regions of the subcontinent.

12

Fruit

Bark

Wonderboom fig (FSA60)   *Ficus salicifolia*

Wonderboomvy

Distribution & habitat The wonderboom fig ranges from the KwaZulu-Natal midlands northwards in the region. It occurs in bushveld, usually on rocky outcrops or in ravines.

Description This shrub or medium-sized evergreen tree occasionally has a spreading crown. The bark is dark grey and the branchlets are hairless. At present, 36 species of fig tree are recognized in southern Africa. Some are characteristic, but others vary to such an extent that expert botanists struggle to identify them with certainty. This species does not pose a problem, as its leaves and figs are characteristic. One well-known example of this species is the enormous wonderboom (wonder tree) at the foot of the Magaliesberg Mountain in Pretoria,

which must be hundreds of years old. The original trunk died long ago but, in 1985, the offspring consisted of 14 groups of stems comprising 72 single stems, each in excess of 100 mm in diameter. In 1984, statistics on this tree were published in the *Journal of Dendrology* 4 (3&4): 172–174, before one of the groups of stems was blown over: girth 16.70 m; height 22 m, spread 53.3 m; cover 2 233 m². **LEAVES** Simple, ovate-oval, dark green, fairly hard, about 70 × 30 mm, folded upwards and distinctly cordate (heart-shaped) at the base. **FLOWERS** Tiny; located inside the fruit. **FRUITS** Small (6 mm in diameter) figs; shiny red when ripe, borne singly or in pairs in the leaf-axils. Although edible, they are not really eaten by humans; however, they are an important food source for birds, monkeys and baboons. **(ZIMBABWE: (Z59) WONDER FIG)**

Above and left: fruit

Sycomore fig (FSA66)   *Ficus sycomorus* subsp. *sycomorus*

Trosvy

Distribution & habitat The sycomore fig is a common sight in and along the rivers of northern KwaZulu-Natal, Swaziland, the Mpumalanga lowveld, Limpopo, Mozambique, Zimbabwe, eastern and northern Botswana and northern and central Namibia.

Description The yellow bark and very thick trunks of large specimens are unmistakable and can be recognized from a distance. Narrow buttresses, which develop at the base of old trunks, are also very characteristic. The *Ficus* genus is thought to have come into existence in the Cretaceous period, more than 100 million years ago. During this time, a fascinating partnership between fig species and a series of wasp species developed, resulting in every fig species now having a specific wasp species as its pollinator. This phenomenon assisted in the classification of the *Ficus* genus. **LEAVES** Large and slightly rough, with entire margins. **FRUITS** Unlike the majority of fig species, fruits are borne in masses on fruiting branchlets, located on the trunk and main branches. Figs are fairly large (up to 40 × 35 mm) and yellow to reddish when ripe; they are an important food source for animals favouring riverine vegetation.

(ZIMBABWE: (Z65) SYCOMORE FIG)

Notes: The tough, pale brown timber is light and soft; it is used for making drums.

Fruit

Water fig (FSA67.1)

Ficus verruculosa

Watervy

Distribution & habitat This is a tropical species, extending as far south as southern Mozambique and northern KwaZulu-Natal. It also occurs intermittently in localized areas further north in Mozambique, as well as Zimbabwe, northern Botswana (Moremi swamps) and the Caprivi area of Namibia.

Description As suggested by its common name, this tree grows only in or near water. The water fig is the chameleon among tree flora on account of its varied growth forms. In gallery forests, it may be a fairly large, sparsely branched tree (12 m), while on the islands in the Okavango Delta, it is a smallish, multi-stemmed, much-branched tree or shrub, forming dense thickets. It seems to be at least semi-deciduous, or possibly deciduous. The bark is quite smooth and pale grey. **LEAVES** Simple, oval to oblong, thick, fairly hard and leathery, glabrous, glossy green above and paler beneath. The underside is sometimes speckled with small encrustations; the margin is rolled under. The conspicuous midrib is mostly yellowish but, as with the petiole, often reddish. **FLOWERS** Male and female flowers are borne inside the figs, as with all fig species. **FRUITS** Small figs, measuring approximately 10 mm in diameter. Figs are borne in pairs in leaf-axils or immediately above leaf scars lower down on the twigs; they are roughly spherical, glabrous, glossy and bright, dark red when mature (January–August). Fruits are tasty and favoured by birds and animals, as are the highly nutritious leaves.

(ZIMBABWE: (Z68) WATER FIG)

Notes: Its bark is valued for its medicinal properties.

Above: fruit
Far left: flowers
Left: young fruit

Wild-almond (FSA72)

Brabejum stellatifolium

Wilde-amandel

Distribution & habitat The wild-almond is restricted to the winter-rainfall area of the Western Cape, where it grows in valleys and often along streams. Shortly after his arrival in the Cape (about 1660), Jan van Riebeeck created a barrier to protect the settlers' cattle against theft. In order to finish the boundary quickly, he ordered the planting of a hedge of wild-almond. Parts of this hedge can still be seen at Kirstenbosch and on Wynberg Hill, pointing to a lifespan of more than 350 years for the species, which is not the case in most other members of the protea family (Proteaceae).

Description It is a smallish tree (up to 8 m) with wide-spreading branches originating low down on the trunk, usually forming a near-impenetrable thicket on the ground. The bark is smooth, sometimes striated, and varies from yellowish grey to pale greyish brown. The wood is fairly hard, light brown and has a reticulated pattern.

LEAVES Very hard with sharply tipped teeth on margins. Leaf arrangement is rather extraordinary: they occur in whorls of four to six, even on fairly thick branches. The species' scientific name refers to this phenomenon.

FLOWERS Small, white, sweetly scented flowers borne in long (up to 80 mm), showy spikes in the axils of the youngest leaves (December–January).

FRUITS Almond-shaped, up to 45 × 30 mm and densely covered with rusty-brown, velvety hairs; young fruits are maroon.

Notes: Due to a lack of large, straight logs, the wood is apparently not put to use.

Above: fruit
Left: fruit

Boekenhout (FSA75)

Faurea saligna

Boekenhout

Distribution & habitat This species occurs from southern KwaZulu-Natal, through Swaziland and into Mpumalanga, where it is widespread from the southern lowveld along the Drakensberg to Limpopo and to the west as far as southern Botswana. It covers most of the inland areas of Zimbabwe, crossing into Mozambique and Malawi.

Description This species occurs most frequently as a smallish tree of 8 m. It is very slender when young; spreading, fairly sparse crown develops with age. Young branchlets are pendent and conspicuously red. Old bark is grey to nearly black and is deeply fissured longitudinally. **LEAVES** Long, narrow and drooping, up to 160 mm long, green to yellowish green and shiny. In younger leaves, petioles and main veins are red. **FLOWERS** Silver-grey with a red tinge, densely packed in cylindrical, pendent spikes up to 150 mm long (August–January, depending on rainfall). During the flowering season, large quantities of nectar are produced. **FRUITS** Small, brown, hairy nuts. (ZIMBABWE: (Z76) WILLOW BEECHWOOD)

Notes: The wood is pale to dark brown with a red tinge and is beautifully figured. It is used for cabinet-making.

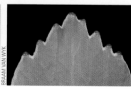

Far left: flowerhead
Left: leaf tip

BRAAM VAN WYK

Green pincushion (FSA84.1) *Leucospermum conocarpodendron* subsp. *viridum*

Groenkreupelhout

Distribution & habitat This is a somewhat rare species which, like most members of the protea family (Proteaceae), is confined to the winter-rainfall region of South Africa. This particular subspecies is restricted to a relatively small area in the Western Cape. The tree illustrated was photographed on the rocky coast near Betty's Bay. The other subspecies (*conocarpodendron*) has an even more limited distribution and is restricted to the Cape Peninsula.

Description *L. conocarpodendron* subsp. *viridum* may be classified as either a shrub or a tree. It can grow to as much as 5 m in height, with branches either at ground level or just above; it has a roundish, umbrella-shaped, fairly dense crown.

It is evergreen. The branches are characteristically crooked and young branches are distinctly hairy. The bark on the branches and trunk is smooth and greyish brown, even on older trees. Of the 47 protea species represented in South Africa, only about seven reach tree size. **LEAVES** Oblong to obovate, up to about 100 × 50 mm, and mostly covered with soft hairs; they are borne close together at the tips of the branches. The basal part of the margin is entire, but a number of prominent teeth occur on either side of the apex; teeth margins may be reddish. **FLOWERS** Large, terminal flowerheads, solitary or in groups of two or three; they consist of a large number of closely packed, bright yellow flowers. Flowering starts in August and may continue into January. **FRUITS** Very small nuts.

Flowerheads

Flowerhead

BRAAM VAN WYK

Common sugarbush (FSA87)

Protea caffra

Gewone suikerbos

Distribution & habitat The most common protea in South Africa. Its range extends from the Katberg mountains in the Eastern Cape, northwards through Lesotho, the Free State (east and north), KwaZulu-Natal, Swaziland, Mpumalanga, Gauteng, Limpopo and eastern parts of North West province, where it occupies most mountains; does not feature in the lowveld of Mpumalanga and Limpopo. It favours well-drained, sandy soils.

Description It occurs most frequently as a single-stemmed tree up to 8 m high, with a short trunk and a sparse, spreading crown. Young branches are smooth and pale grey. The fissured bark is dark grey to black and breaks up into small blocks. Large specimens may be up to 100 years old. **LEAVES** Usually linear-elliptic, up to 250 mm long, glabrous, greyish green, thick, hard and covered with silvery hairs. **FLOWERS** Flowerheads borne solitarily and terminally (December–January), mainly pink or carmine with green at the base, though forms with creamy-green bracts are also found. They have a pleasant, sweet odour. **FRUITS** Small nuts.

Notes: It grows slowly, but this tree is highly recommended as a garden subject; it should start flowering at about five years of age.

Flowerheads

Forest white sugarbush (FSA93)

Protea mundii

Boswitsuikerbos

Distribution & habitat This tree has a rather curious distribution. It predominantly occupies the area between George and the Groendal Wilderness area in the Strydomsberg, near Uitenhage, in southeastern South Africa and is abundant over this range, which includes the Tsitsikamma area. About 300 km to the west, between Hermanus and Betty's Bay, several isolated populations flourish, with no recorded occurrence anywhere between these two ranges.

Description Inclusion of at least one of the proteas is an absolute necessity for any publication dealing with woody vegetation – whether trees or shrubs – in southern Africa. The choice of this species was facilitated by the fact that it is considered to be the tallest growing of all the arborescent proteas in South Africa. This is usually a smallish, upright, slender tree measuring up to approximately 8 m in height, though it may reach as much as 12 m. The main trunk is short, as it subdivides near the ground; branches are long and upright. The bark is smooth and greyish brown. **LEAVES** Narrowly elliptic to elliptic, up to 120 mm long, pale green and distinctly veined, with a typically reddish midrib. **FLOWERS** Flowerheads up to 80 mm long, they have silky green bracts (bracts may also be pink) fringed with hairs; they do not open wide. Flowering begins in midsummer and may continue until the following spring. **FRUITS** Small nuts covered in hair-like outgrowths.

Notes: Although it was collected by Burchell in 1814, it was named in honour of Leopold Mund, who arrived at the Cape in 1815 to collect plants for the Berlin Museum.

Flowers

Fruit

Tanninbush (FSA99)

Osyris compressa

Pruimbas

Distribution & habitat Only two tree species in the sandalwood family (Santalaceae) are present in southern Africa: *O. compressa* and *O. lanceolata* (rock tanninbush). As the latter is cold resistant, it is widespread from the Eastern Cape through the Free State, Lesotho and into the northern provinces of South Africa. It is also found in all other countries of the subcontinent. The tanninbush is widespread from the Western Cape all along the coast to northern KwaZulu-Natal and into southern Mozambique. It is mostly confined to coastal dunes, but may also occur fairly far inland.

Description In fairly open fynbos areas on coastal dunes, it is a very dense, spreading, multi-stemmed, small tree (3–4 m) with its branches on the ground. Stems have fairly smooth, brownish grey bark. **LEAVES** Smallish (up to 50 mm long), elliptic, leathery, hard, sharply tipped and dull green with a grey bloom; they are borne close together in opposite pairs. **FLOWERS** Tiny, inconspicuous and yellowish green, they are borne in compact, terminal heads. Flowering takes place over a very long period, probably March–September; flowers and mature fruit are usually found together. **FRUITS** Oval, up to 15 mm long and often closely packed; initially shiny red, changing to purplish black when mature.

Notes: Due to high tannin content, the leaves and bark have been used for the tanning of hides.

Flowers

Fruit

Green-apple (FSA107)

Monodora junodii

Groenappel

Distribution & habitat This is a tropical species with an easterly distribution. It is found along the Zambezi in Mozambique, in eastern Zimbabwe and in the northeastern corner of Limpopo; isolated populations occur at the southern tip of Mozambique and Maputaland in KwaZulu-Natal. It usually grows in dense thickets in deep sand and occasionally on rocky outcrops.

Description It is a multi-stemmed, deciduous, slender plant with long, thin, supple branches. The bark is dark greyish brown and smooth. **LEAVES** Exceptionally glossy, bright green, oblanceolate to nearly elliptic, up to 150 mm long and borne alternately. **FLOWERS** Showy, beautiful and unusual, they are borne solitarily near the ends of branches (September–November). They consist of three sepals and six petals, in two whorls of three. Those at the base (the outer whorl) are broad, flat, spreading and bent either backwards or forwards; those in the inner whorl stand upright, close together and are cupped and clawed. Different colour variations occur. **FRUITS** Reminiscent of the custard-apple; they are nearly spherical, dark green, mottled with white and up to 70 mm in diameter. At maturity, they turn brownish black and wrinkled. (ZIMBABWE: (Z109) GREEN-APPLE)

22

Flowers

Fruit

River dwababerry (FSA108)   *Friesodielsia obovata*

Rivierdwababessie

Distribution & habitat In order to see this species, one must visit the far northern part of Botswana, the Caprivi Strip or the northern, eastern and northwestern areas of Zimbabwe. It is also known to occur in the northwestern part of Mozambique. Although the river dwababerry grows in fairly divergent habitats, it seems to thrive in dense woodland on well-drained sand, as is evident by the fact that dense thickets often develop here.

Description This tree belongs to the custard-apple family (Annonaceae), most members of which are noted for their extraordinary, very brightly coloured, edible fruit. It is most often encountered as a shrub or a scrambler, but may grow to about 7 m. Nearly all plants are multi-stemmed, with the branch-ends resting on the ground. The bark is grey and fairly smooth. **LEAVES** Simple, markedly obovate to nearly rectangular, thin, fairly large (mostly about 80 × 50 mm) and always velvety when young, while only occasionally velvety when mature. **FLOWERS** Inconspicuous and cream-coloured, they are borne solitarily and have thick, rather fleshy sepals and petals (November–December). **FRUITS** Characteristic and attractive, red, fleshy, edible; they are cylindrical, measure up to about 80 mm in length and are constricted between the seeds. They occur in bunches that are reminiscent of a hand, or of miniature sausages strung together. Primates, birds and insects relish them.

(**ZIMBABWE:** (Z98) NORTHERN DWABABERRY)

Flowers

Fruit

Propellertree (FSA120)

Gyrocarpus americanus subsp. *africanus*

Helikopterboom

Distribution & habitat This tree occurs in the north of Namibia and Mozambique, the north and south of Zimbabwe and in South Africa at the Soutpansberg and Crook's Corner in northeastern Limpopo. It prefers a rocky substrate and is found on hillsides or ridges.

Description It is a smallish tree (8 m), but may reach 15 m, with a sparse, spreading, more-or-less rounded crown. This tree always has a single, tall, bare, exceptionally smooth and shiny trunk. On its shady side, the bark is usually pale grey to grey-brown, but on the sunny side, it is generally bleached almost white. **LEAVES** Simple and measuring 100 × 100 mm; older leaves have three lobes. **FLOWERS** Small and yellow, they are borne in terminal racemes; each contains several male and fewer female flowers in autumn. **FRUITS** Borne in pendent clusters, changing colour from light green through yellow to dark brown. Each consists of a very hard, oval fruit about 20 mm in length, with two stiff, narrow, papery wings about 70 mm in length. When the ripe fruit falls in July–August, the weight of the nut turns it around and the wings cause it to spin as it floats down. (ZIMBABWE: (Z114) PROPELLERTREE)

Left: fruit
Above: flowers

Shepherd's tree (FSA122)

Boscia albitrunca

Witgat

Distribution & habitat It occurs throughout Namibia, southern Mozambique, the southern and western parts of western Zimbabwe and all the northern provinces of South Africa, except the eastern Highveld, including the Northern Cape, the western Free State, Swaziland and some areas in KwaZulu-Natal. Although it has a widespread distribution, this tree seems to prefer arid conditions. It occurs on a variety of soil types, from sand to clay and even rocky locations in open or fairly dense woodland.

Description While it may reach a height of 10 m in an ideal situation, it is usually only 5–7 m high. It is a single-stemmed tree with a small, rather dense, twiggy crown.

The branches are very smooth and almost white; the stem is smooth and occasionally grooved. It is evergreen to deciduous. Bark, which peels in small sections, may be smooth and almost white or greyish brown. **LEAVES** Small, simple and borne singly or in small groups on abbreviated lateral twigs. They are thick, hard, brittle and slightly scabrid. **FLOWERS** Greenish yellow, minute and borne in racemes in such great quantities along the twigs and thicker branches that the tree is quite imposing in full bloom (usually October–December, but sometimes later). **FRUITS** Spherical, smooth and yellow to pale red when ripe. If conditions are right, large quantities are produced. They are edible and are relished by birds.

(ZIMBABWE: (Z121) SHEPHERD'S TREE)

Top: fruit
Above: flowers

Beadbean (FSA132) *Maerua angolensis* subsp. *angolensis*

Knoppiesboontjie

Distribution & habitat Despite its wide distribution on the subcontinent, the beadbean is not really abundant anywhere. Because individual specimens usually occur very far apart in South Africa, it is therefore one of the lesser-known components of the local tree flora.

Description It may reach about 15 m in height, but is usually not more than about 6 m. It has a single, bare trunk and a moderately spreading, sparse crown. Although one leafless tree has been found, the beadbean is probably evergreen. Old stems are grey-brown with a red-brown tinge. The bark has shallow grooves and

peels off in small, powdery flakes, exposing the bright green living bark. **LEAVES** Simple and borne spirally at twig terminals. The most characteristic part of the leaf is the petiole, which is reddish brown, bent at a distinct angle near its conjunction with the leaf and cylindrically thickened at both ends. **FLOWERS** Like most members of the caper family (Capparaceae), petals are absent; the most obvious components of its attractive flowers are long, brilliantly white stamens, which turn yellow when withering (September–October). They are borne solitarily and axillary. **FRUITS** Cylindrical and conspicuously deeply segmented, resembling a pod.

(ZIMBABWE: (Z131) BEADBEAN)

Left: flowers
Above: fruit

Mobolaplum (FSA146)

Parinari curatellifolia

Grysappel

Distribution & habitat One of the major wild fruit trees in southern Africa, the mobolaplum is left untouched by the locals when bush is cleared for crops. It is widespread throughout most of Zimbabwe; also found in the Limpopo and Mpumalanga lowveld, Swaziland, the Caprivi Strip and northern Mozambique. It only grows on deep, well-drained sandy soils.

Description Reputed to reach a height of 24 m, although most information indicates an average height of roughly half that size. It is a single-stemmed tree with a short, bare trunk and a dense, wide-spreading crown characterized by drooping branch ends. It is practically evergreen. The bark is rough and dark grey, although in areas where veld fires frequently occur, the bark is always black. **LEAVES** Simple, hard, brittle, measuring 90 × 50 mm. Older leaves are dark green, glossy and glabrous on the upper side; the undersides are covered with an off-white or rust-coloured downy layer. The secondary veins are arranged in a herringbone pattern. **FLOWERS** The small, white flowers are borne in large, axillary or terminal panicles (October–November). **FRUITS** Oval, up to 30 mm long, edible and sweetly flavoured; pulp is yellowish when fruits are ripe (August–September).

(ZIMBABWE: (Z149) MOBOLAPLUM)

Top: fruit
Above: flowers

Flatcrown (FSA148)

Albizia adianthifolia var. *adianthifolia*

Platkroon

Distribution & habitat This tropical tree species is widespread in central Africa, but on the subcontinent occurs only in the east – namely in Mozambique, the eastern and southeastern parts of Zimbabwe, the Limpopo and Mpumalanga lowveld, and along the coast of KwaZulu-Natal and the Eastern Cape. It is prominent in coastal regions.

Description The common name is apt, as most of the full-grown trees have the same unmistakable, wide-spreading and mostly flat crown supported by a long, straight, bare trunk. It is deciduous, but is densely covered with leaves during summer. The biggest trees usually encountered are about 18 m high, though Palgrave (2005) mentions a maximum height of 40 m. **LEAVES** Bipinnately compound and up to 250 mm long. **FLOWERS** Emerge in spring, after the new leaves, borne in dense heads at the tips of twigs. They are less attractive than those of most other *Albizia* species. **FRUITS** Fairly long (150 × 25 mm), flat pods; biscuit-coloured to pale brown when mature. They are dehiscent and only reach maturity in the autumn of the following year.

(ZIMBABWE: (Z153) ROUGH-BARKED FLATCROWN)

Notes: Although the wood is relatively soft and light, it is suitable for the manufacture of furniture as well as parquet flooring.

Flowers

Fruit

Bushveld false-thorn (FSA155)

Albizia harveyi

Bosveldvalsdoring

Distribution & habitat This is a tropical species, found throughout Africa from Swaziland to Tanzania, including the Mpumalanga and Limpopo lowveld, eastern and northern Botswana, northeastern Namibia and various parts of Zimbabwe and Mozambique. It grows on a variety of soil types, but more and larger trees are found on low-lying alluvial soils and brackish plains.

Description Although often encountered as a small, very sparse, multi-stemmed shrub, this tree can reach a height of 16 m, as shown in the picture. That particular tree's trunk girth at breast height is 4.1 m. The trunk usually branches fairly low and the somewhat dense crown is wide-spreading. It is deciduous. Old stems are dark grey and the rough bark cracks into prominent, vertical ridges, which fuse at random intervals. **LEAVES** Feathery, bipinnately compound and fairly long and narrow (150 × 50 mm). The leaflets are grey-green, small (60 × 20 mm) and slightly sickle-shaped. **FLOWERS** Small, white and borne in rather loose, fluffy heads, with or just after the young leaves (October–November). As with other *Albizia* species, the stamens are the most important and visible component of the flowers. **FRUITS** Pale brown, pergamentaceous, thin, flat and oblong pods, up to 130 mm long and 30 mm wide. Masses of pendent pods are produced, either singly or in small bunches.

(ZIMBABWE: (Z161) SICKLE-LEAVED FALSE-THORN)

Notes: The timber is medium-heavy, pale brown and finely textured; it produces a smooth finish but is not used for any large-scale commercial purposes.

Top: flowers
Above: fruit

Large-leaved false-thorn (FSA158)   *Albizia versicolor*

Grootblaarvalsdoring

Distribution & habitat This tropical species occurs roughly from northern Namibia, eastwards into the Caprivi Strip and northern Botswana, and along the Zambezi River to the Indian Ocean. From northeastern Zimbabwe and northern Mozambique it extends southwards through the Limpopo and Mpumalanga lowveld into Swaziland and northern KwaZulu-Natal. It shows a preference for moist conditions and is often found in low-lying areas near watercourses, in areas with a relatively high rainfall and/or deep, sandy soil and in fairly open woodland.

Description It is a medium to large deciduous tree (up to 18 m) with a single, straight, long trunk and a dense, wide-spreading crown. Young twigs are covered with golden-brown hairs. Old stems are rough and dark grey; the bark peels off in small, flat sections. **LEAVES** Large (about 300 × 200 mm) and bipinnately compound. New leaflets are dark reddish brown, while old ones are green to slightly dark green. Leaflets are big (up to 55 × 35 mm) and vary from broadly elliptic to almost rectangular. **FLOWERS** Powderpuff-like inflorescences are large and white but wither quickly, becoming yellow (November–December or later). **FRUITS** Thin, flat, oblong (up to 200 × 50 mm), glabrous and smooth pods; they change from green to yellowish green to wine-red and finally pale brown.

(ZIMBABWE: (Z165) POISONPOD FALSE-THORN)

Flowers

Fruit

Anatree (FSA159)   *Faidherbia albida*

Anaboom

Distribution & habitat This tree occurs in the warmer, mostly frost-free areas of South Africa, from northern KwaZulu-Natal through the Mpumalanga lowveld to the northern parts of Limpopo. It is relatively rare in Botswana, but is fairly abundant in the northwestern parts of Namibia and the extreme northern region of Zimbabwe. Although accustomed to a mild climate, it can withstand very low temperatures. It grows mostly on the banks of rivers and other watercourses.

Description This species has recently been removed from the *Acacia* genus and is now the only species in the genus *Faidherbia*. One aspect in which it differs markedly from the acacias is that it sheds its leaves in summer. **LEAVES** Bipinnately compound and bluish green; new leaves emerge immediately after the summer leaves are shed, meaning that the tree is in full leaf in winter. **FLOWERS** White, borne in long spikes; emerge in autumn, which is an unusual time relative to most African trees. **FRUITS** Large, attractively coloured pods; they are well known for their nutritional value.
(ZIMBABWE: (Z212) ALBIDA)

Notes: The public's attention was drawn to this tree by the famous South African author Eugène Marais, who wrote about the gigantic trees on the bank of the Magalakwin River in northwestern Limpopo, which he first saw in 1908.

Left: flowers
Above: fruit

Camel thorn (FSA168)   *Acacia erioloba*

Kameeldoring

Distribution & habitat The camel thorn is undoubtedly the king of trees in the arid western regions of southern Africa; it also occurs in central and southern Limpopo, the southwestern part of Zimbabwe and the northern area of Botswana (where rainfall is relatively high). In the northwestern part of the Northern Cape and the North West province, it is often the dominant tree on plains, sometimes occurring in dense, isolated clumps. This tree has a widespread distribution in a variety of ecological situations, though it tends to prefer sandy soil. In very arid areas, it grows almost exclusively in riverbeds or on riverbanks. Trees occurring outside this favoured habitat are usually stunted.

Description Although gigantic trees (height 18 m, girth 9 m) have been reported from the Kuiseb River in Namibia, they generally only reach 9–10 m in height. The bark is rough and longitudinally fissured. The shiny, initially dark brown and later grey, swollen, straight thorns are characteristic and are found in pairs. **LEAVES** Small and bipinnately compound. **FLOWERS** Characteristically bright yellow spherical inflorescences (August–September). **FRUITS** Pods, which are usually very broad, thick, sickle-shaped, grey and velvety. They are indehiscent. Variations occur in the shape and size of the pods (some are thin, round and long).
(**ZIMBABWE:** (Z177) CAMEL THORN)

Notes: This is a valuable evergreen tree, especially in the hot, dry western areas, because it provides shade throughout the year. The leaves and pods, which are rich in protein, sustain a variety of wild animals and domestic stock.

Left: flowers
Top: fruit subsp. hebeclada
Above: fruit subsp. tristis

Candlepod thorn (FSA170)

Acacia hebeclada subsp. *hebeclada*

Trassiedoring

Distribution & habitat Found in the arid western regions of the subcontinent, including the Northern Cape, North West province, northern, eastern and southern Botswana and large parts of Namibia.

Description This tree is extraordinary for two reasons: 1. The pods stand upright, unlike most other pods, which are pendent. This applies to subspecies *chobiensis*, but not to *tristis*; 2. The major subspecies, *hebeclada*, although a true tree-like plant that branches low in some cases, occurs more often as a dense thicket and may assume very large proportions as new plants sprout from the roots around the mother plant. The largest of these, included in the *National Register of Big Trees*, has the dimensions: girth of all stems in total 6.06 m; height 7 m; spread 55.6 m and cover 2 431 m^2. This tree grows in the Waterberg area of Limpopo, which has a relatively high rainfall. In the main distribution area, this tree can assume the same spread and cover as the specimen above, but will be only 1–2 m high. The bark is rough and longitudinally fissured. Thorns, found in pairs below the nodes, are straight, recurved or straight with recurved tips.

LEAVES Bipinnately compound. **FLOWERS** Small, off-white, spherical inflorescences are produced from July to September. **FRUITS** Long, straight, thick, hard, brown pods covered with yellowish hairs.

(ZIMBABWE: (Z187) CANDLEPOD THORN; NAMIBIA: CANDLEPOD ACACIA)

Notes: The San build their shelters in the middle of these thickets to protect themselves from lions and other predators.

Bark

Fruit

Fungus gall

Flowers

Sweet thorn (FSA172)

Acacia karroo

Soetdoring

Distribution & habitat It can be found throughout South Africa, with the exception of the Gordonia area in the Northern Cape, coastal parts of the Eastern Cape and KwaZulu-Natal and extreme eastern parts of Limpopo and Mpumalanga. It also covers the greater parts of Namibia and Zimbabwe. In Botswana, it is limited to the eastern, southeastern and northern regions; it is essentially absent from Mozambique. Sweet thorns occur on a variety of soil types and in a variety of habitats. In a number of areas, such as the Karoo, Namibia and northwestern Limpopo, it is most often encountered in the low-lying areas with clay-like soil, next to watercourses.

Description This is one of the most common trees in the greater part of the subcontinent. It has therefore adapted to large fluctuations in temperature and moisture. This species varies considerably in growth form. In the Karoo, the Free State and the North West province, it is generally a smallish tree with a short trunk and spreading crown. In other areas, such as Limpopo and Mpumalanga, it is a long, slender tree. In all areas, it often occurs in dense, nearly homogeneous stands. The bark is smooth and brownish grey, however, on old specimens it becomes black and longitudinally fissured. **LEAVES** Dark green and bipinnately compound. **FLOWERS** Beautiful, dark yellow, spherical flowerheads appear mostly in November–December, though sometimes as late as March. **FRUITS** Sickle-shaped, dehiscent pods that remain on the tree for a year or more. (ZIMBABWE: (Z189) SWEET THORN)

Left: fruit
Above: flowers

Umbrella thorn (FSA188)   *Acacia tortilis* subsp. *heteracantha*

Haak-en-steek

Distribution & habitat Two distinct subspecies of this tree occur in southern Africa. The subspecies *heteracantha* is widespread across the subcontinent and is adapted to a wide range of climatic conditions.

Description It is deciduous and usually not more than 10 m high. In northern Botswana (Moremi), some trees reach 20 m. The well-known, conspicuous, umbrella-shaped crown is only fully developed in old specimens; young trees have roundish or flat-topped crowns. The stem is usually fairly short and the main branches are bare. Old bark is dark grey to black and fairly deeply, longitudinally fissured and ridged. The very sharp spines of this plant are unique: some are short, blackish and hooked, while others are long, white and straight (the species name refers to the spines). Spines occur in pairs: mostly two of the same kind together, but sometimes mixed (i.e. a hooked and a straight spine paired together). All parts are without hairs. **LEAVES** Bipinnately compound and probably the smallest among the thorn trees (30 × 15 mm). The same applies to leaflets, which are minute (1.5 × 0.5 mm). **FLOWERS** Globose inflorescences consisting of a fairly large number of small, white flowers, which are packed together; they are borne in groups among the leaves, usually in November–December. **FRUITS** Characteristic, pale brown pods that are always spirally contorted and sometimes intertwined.

(ZIMBABWE: (Z208) UMBRELLA THORN)

Notes: The heartwood of umbrella thorn is reddish brown, very hard and fairly heavy. It is seldom used, except as firewood. The leaves and highly nutritious pods are widely foraged by a variety of animals, including domestic stock. The pods are mainly utilized during winter, after they have fallen to the ground.

Left: flowers
Top: bark
Above: fruit

Fever tree (FSA189)

Acacia xanthophloea

Koorsboom

Distribution & habitat This tree has a markedly eastern distribution in southern Africa, from northern KwaZulu-Natal through Swaziland, Mozambique, the eastern part of the Mpumalanga and Limpopo lowveld, the Zimbabwe lowveld and further north. It grows in low-lying, fairly wet to swampy areas, and may occur in very dense stands.

Description Fever trees are known worldwide, possibly as a result of Rudyard Kipling's story about the elephant's child, who continued travelling northwards until at last he came 'to the banks of the great, grey-green, greasy Limpopo River, all set about with fever trees'. It is an unusual, striking, medium-large, deciduous tree (up to 15 m) with a long, single stem and wide-spreading crown. The bark of old stems is very smooth, yellow-green and powdery, with conspicuous longitudinal indentations. Its long, white thorns are straight, smooth, sharp and are borne in pairs. LEAVES Bipinnately compound, rather small and occur in small groups immediately above the thorns. FLOWERS Fragrant, golden-yellow, round inflorescences are borne among the leaves (August–September). FRUITS Pods, up to 100 mm long.

(ZIMBABWE: (Z211) FEVERTREE THORN)

Notes: The timber is pale brown with a reddish tinge and is quite hard and heavy; it can be used for carpentry.

Left: fruit & seeds
Above: flowers

Lebombo-wattle (FSA191)

Newtonia hildebrandtii var. *hildebrandtii*

Lebombowattel

Distribution & habitat In South Africa, this species occurs mainly in KwaZulu-Natal. Literally dozens of beautiful specimens grow in the sandveld next to the road in Kosi Bay, east of the Pongola River. The only other area where it occurs is in the Lebombo mountain range, immediately north of the Olifants River in the Kruger National Park – an area that is inaccessible to the general public. It also features fairly widely in Mozambique, as well as southeastern Zimbabwe and isolated patches further north.

Description It is a large (up to 25 m), deciduous tree with a wide-spreading, dense crown and a relatively short, bare trunk. The branch-ends are pendent. Old stems are dark grey; the bark peels off in strips and small blocks. **LEAVES** Bipinnately compound, fairly small (90 mm long) and dark green. A small, brown gland occurs on the rachis between each pair of pinnae. **FLOWERS** Small, white flowers, which are grouped together in fairly long (80 mm), axillary spikes. They are produced in large quantities, typically in November–December, depending on rainfall. **FRUITS** Exceptionally flat, long pods of about 300 mm, which are initially dark red and later brown to black. The seeds are unique: very thin, flat and surrounded by a reddish brown papery wing. Pods split (on one side only) to release the seeds, which remain attached to the pod for months on end.

(ZIMBABWE: (Z217) LEBOMBO-WATTLE)

Notes: The timber is hard, heavy and dark brown to black. It is of good quality, and should be suitable for cabinet-making.

Fruit

Flowers

Tip of branchlet

Wild-seringa (FSA197)

Burkea africana

Wildesering

Distribution & habitat The wild-seringa occurs in the northern provinces of South Africa, from Johannesburg northwards throughout Zimbabwe, in large areas of Mozambique, the northern and southeastern regions of Botswana and northern Namibia.

Description This is a deciduous tree. The leaves, which are close together at the twig terminals, are confined to the treetops. The young twigs are distinctly rust-coloured due to a dense cover of hairs. Old bark is dark grey and subdivided into small blocks. The durable timber is hard, tough and pale red to red-brown. This is probably the tree featured in many of the paintings of the famous South

African artist Pierneef, whose works depict trees with distinctive long, bare trunk and comparatively small, spreading, flat-topped crown. Some wild-seringas do not comply with this description, such as the example in the Makopane district, which has a fairly short trunk and a wide-spreading crown (23.5 m diameter), as measured by the Dendrological Society. **LEAVES** Bipinnately compound with two (sometimes three) pairs of pinnae. **FLOWERS** Small, sweet-smelling, white to creamy and grouped together in single, long (250 mm) spikes borne in leaf-axils (October–November). **FRUITS** Smallish, smooth, flat, hard, woody and single-seeded; they consist of many pods in pendent clusters. (ZIMBABWE: (Z229) MUKARATI; NAMIBIA: BURKEA)

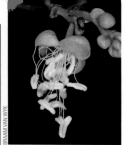
Flower

Fruit

Mopane (FSA198)   *Colophospermum mopane*

Mopanie

Distribution & habitat The mopane dominates the African vegetation over large tracts of land. In southern Africa, this applies to the middle section of northern Namibia, the Caprivi Strip, northeastern Botswana, the west, south and north of Zimbabwe, large areas in central Mozambique, as well as the northern and northeastern parts of Limpopo – especially in the Kruger National Park – and north of the Soutpansberg. It usually dominates the vegetation to such an extent that it is often found in dense, nearly homogeneous stands.

Description Under favourable soil and climatic conditions, as in Moremi National Park in Botswana, it grows into a large tree (20 m) with a thickset stem and long, bare branches. In contrast, the plants in the northeastern section of the Kruger National Park are multi-stemmed shrubs, which barely reach 2 m. The wood is hard, heavy and mainly dark brown to nearly black. **LEAVES** Two leaflets (mirror images of each other) on a common petiole, creating the look of butterfly wings. **FLOWERS** Small, yellowish green and inconspicuous (December–January). **FRUITS** Flat pods (50 × 25 mm) that are half-moon-shaped, wrinkled and biscuit-coloured when ripe. Seeds have small, reddish glands, which exude a sticky fluid on both surfaces. (ZIMBABWE: (Z230) MOPANE)

Top: flowers
Above left: young leaves
Above right: fruit

Mufuti, Prince-of-Wales' feathers (FSA198.2)   *Brachystegia boehmii*

Mufuti

Distribution & habitat In southern Africa, most *Brachystegia* species are found in Zimbabwe and Mozambique. Of these, only *B. boehmii* has become established in Botswana (in the Kasane area in the northeast). Together with *Julbernardia globiflora* and *B. tamarindoides* subsp. *microphylla*, the two *Brachystegia* species mentioned here largely dominate the highveld vegetation in central Zimbabwe.

Description With one exception, all *Brachystegia* species have a true tree form: a single, long trunk and a wide-spreading crown. Because of its local abundance, beautiful shape and the deep red colouring of young leaves, the musasa (*B. spiciformis*) is the best known of its genus. Prince-of-Wales' feathers is a very attractive, large, deciduous tree, which can measure in excess of 15 m. It earned its common name from the striking colours (often bright red) of the large leaf buds and leaves. **LEAVES** Old leaves are feathery and greyish green. **FLOWERS** Somewhat inconspicuous, they are greenish white, sweetly scented and borne in short axillary or terminal spikes (September–December). **FRUITS** Panga-shaped pods, which are hard, woody and covered with dark brown hairs, especially when young. They split open while still on the tree, explosively scattering seeds.

(ZIMBABWE: (Z234) MUFUTI, PRINCE-OF-WALES' FEATHERS)

Flowers

Fruit & seeds

Large copalwood (FSA199)

Guibourtia coleosperma

Grootvalsmopanie

Distribution & habitat This genus is represented by two tree species on the subcontinent of southern Africa. The smaller one, *G. conjugata*, is widespread and deciduous whereas *G. coleosperma* occurs only in the northeastern area of Namibia and the extreme north of Botswana, spreading southeastwards along the Zimbabwe-Botswana border. **Description** It is generally evergreen. It can grow up to 20 m high; it is an impressive, single-stemmed tree with a wide-spreading crown. Young branches are reddish, becoming conspicuously cream-coloured with dark brown to black patches of flaking bark. The bark of old trunks is slightly yellowish grey or can become dark blackish brown. The Zimbabwean common name refers to the fact that the identical, sickle-shaped pairs of leaflets resemble those of the mopane. **FLOWERS** Smallish, white, star-shaped flowers borne in fairly large, terminal panicles (December–April). **FRUITS** Characteristic, small, almost circular (up to 30 mm long), flat but thickened pods, which turn brown when mature. When ripe, they split on one side and the two valves curl back to release a single, shiny, red seed, which has a bright scarlet aril on one side that is attached to a thread-like stalk. Seeds and arils are widely used as food.
(ZIMBABWE: (Z231) LARGE FALSE-MOPANE, UMTSHIBI)

Notes: The wood is commercially utilized and is known as muchibi. It is attractive, rather soft and pinkish brown.

Far left: flowers
Left: fruit

Karoo boerbean (FSA201)

Schotia afra var. *afra*

Karooboerboon

Distribution & habitat Four species belonging to the genus *Schotia* (one with two subspecies) occur in southern Africa. *S. latifolia* grows only in the Eastern Cape and a small area in Sekhukhuneland (around Burgersfort). *S. capitata* is usually a component of dense thickets in KwaZulu-Natal, Swaziland, southeastern Mpumalanga, southern Mozambique and southern Zimbabwe. The larger *S. brachypetala* has an eastern distribution from the Eastern Cape to the north of Zimbabwe. *S. afra* var. *afra* is very common in arid regions of the Western and Eastern Cape.

Description This boerbean is a small (up to 5 m), particularly dense, evergreen tree, often with a twisted trunk and smooth, pale grey branches and twigs, which are very stiff. Old trunks have dark grey bark, which remains fairly smooth. **LEAVES** Paripinnately compound and feathery. Leaflets are small, linear and dark green. **FLOWERS** Bright red (rarely, petals will be pink) with a waxy appearance, they are striking and borne in dense clusters. Flowering takes place in spring (August–October), depending on rainfall. **FRUITS** Bunches of large, flat, twisted, colourful pods, each encircled by a distinctive rim, which become woody and brown when mature. They remain hanging on the tree when the two flat sides break loose at ripening. The pale brown seeds are slightly flattened and roundish, with a very small or absent aril.

Flowers

Fruit

Zambezi-teak (FSA206)

Baikiaea plurijuga

Zambezikiaat

Distribution & habitat Currently-available distribution data show this tree in the northern and northeastern regions of Namibia, northern Botswana and the western, southwestern and central areas of Zimbabwe. It prefers the deep Kalahari sand, which is the dominant soil type in its distribution areas; it is found mainly in fairly open woodland.

Description It has a single, straight trunk and a dense, wide-spreading crown, which is mostly roundish at the top; the outer branches often hang low. The bark is smooth and pale grey on young branches, becoming grey-brown and vertically fissured in old specimens, which may be up to 15 m in height. An outstanding feature of the Zambezi teak is the fact that the large inflorescences (up to 300 mm long) stand upright and can therefore be clearly seen above the canopy. **LEAVES** Pinnately compound with four or five pairs of opposite leaflets. **FLOWERS** Each inflorescence (a raceme) consists of a large number of flowers arranged in two rows on either side of the peduncle. They are fairly large, with four striking purple petals and one pale purple to nearly white petal. Flowers at the base of the inflorescence open first and, as only one or two flowers open simultaneously, the flowering period is extended (usually December–March). **FRUITS** Thick, hairy, woody pods that split open, while on the trees, to release the seeds.

(ZIMBABWE: (Z241) ZAMBEZI-TEAK)

Notes: The high-quality wood is reddish brown, finely textured and durable. It is used for furniture, flooring and even railway sleepers.

Top: flowers & fruit
Above: fruit & seeds

Pod-mahogany (FSA207) *Afzelia quanzensis*

Peulmahonie

Distribution & habitat This magnificent tropical species is relatively widespread in southern Africa, growing in the eastern areas from northern KwaZulu-Natal and Swaziland, through the Mpumalanga lowveld, across northeastern Limpopo to Zimbabwe and over large areas of Mozambique, the northeastern tip of Botswana and the eastern part of the Caprivi Strip.

Description It is a single-stemmed, deciduous tree with an unusually wide-spreading, sometimes umbrella-like crown. Although it does not often exceed 12 m in height, Palgrave (2005) states that in ideal conditions it can reach 35 m. **LEAVES** Pinnately compound and up to 400 mm long (mostly 150 mm). **FLOWERS** Extraordinarily, they have only one petal, which is large and red with yellow veining or red speckles. Flowering can commence in August but is usually in October–November. **FRUITS** Large pods (200 × 70 mm) are half-moon-shaped, flat, thick, woody and dark brown. They split on the tree to release seeds, which are oblong, shiny and black, with a scarlet to orange aril enveloping one end. Seeds are often strung into necklaces or other trinkets and sold as curios. (ZIMBABWE: (Z243) POD-MAHOGANY)

Notes: The wood is well-known in the furniture trade and is sold under the trade name chamfuta.

Flowers

Fruit

Munondo (FSA207.1)

Julbernardia globiflora

Dubbelkroonboom

Distribution & habitat This is the only *Julbernardia* species occurring in Zimbabwe and Botswana and Mozambique. The other southern African species, *J. paniculata,* has a limited distribution in Mozambique, occurring north of Beira only. Six other species occur in tropical Africa north of the Zambezi. This particular species can be found throughout Zimbabwe; it does not enter South Africa and apparently has an eastern distribution in Africa. It is co-dominant with *Brachystegia spiciformis* over large areas of Zimbabwe, Mozambique and countries such as Tanzania and the Democratic Republic of Congo, with a limited distribution in the northeast of Botswana and the Caprivi Strip.

Description It is a magnificent, single-stemmed, deciduous tree of up to 16 m in height. According to Palgrave (2005), it is an ecologically important species. **LEAVES** Young leaves are soft pink or fawn, as opposed to those of *B. spiciformis* (whose young leaves are pink to intensely red) with which *J. globiflora* may be confused. **FLOWERS** White, fairly small and borne in large (up to 300 mm long), loose, terminal heads. They appear from January to May and are dropped soon after opening. **FRUITS** Pods are large, dark brown, velvety and crown the tree. They open while on the tree, explosively releasing seeds.

(ZIMBABWE: (Z244) MUNONDO)

Notes: The wood is hard, coarse and very durable. Palgrave (2005) states that it is difficult to work, with a tendency to tear when sawn and split badly when nailed; it is used quite widely as a general-purpose timber.

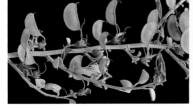

Left: fruit
Above: flowers

Butterflyleaf (FSA208)

Adenolobus garipensis

Gariepbauhinia

Distribution & habitat Its distribution in the arid northwestern area of the Cape and central Namibia, as far as the Kunene River, proves that it is both drought-resistant as well as frost-tolerant. It can therefore be cultivated in most areas of the subcontinent.

Description It is a multi-stemmed plant with smooth greyish bark on young branches, turning dark grey and developing longitudinal ridges when old. The crown is sparse and only slightly spreading with long, slender, trailing branchlets. This is not a particularly impressive tree, as it reaches only 5 m in height, but several of its other characteristics justify closer attention by gardeners.

LEAVES Simple, bluish green, smallish and two-lobed, like those of the plants in the *Bauhinia* genus, to which it belonged until reclassified.

FLOWERS Beautifully coloured, but not spectacular, they are tubular and up to 25 mm in length. Petals are greyish with maroon net veining, the calyx is maroon-red and stamens are conspicuous. A flowering time of September–January has been reported, but all evidence points to a longer flowering season, possibly from the end of winter through to the following autumn. **FRUITS** Pods are a beautiful reddish colour when young; they are half-moon-shaped, flat and dotted with glands.

Notes: The wood is used only as firewood.

Left: fruit
Above: flowers

Kalahari bauhinia (FSA208.3) *Bauhinia petersiana* subsp. *macrantha*

Kalaharibauhinia

Distribution & habitat This species has a somewhat more westerly distribution on the subcontinent than most South African trees. From the Northern Cape, its range extends northwards through the eastern side of Botswana into Zimbabwe and westwards through northern Botswana and the Caprivi Strip into northern Namibia. It is abundant in the deep sandy soil of the Chobe/Kasane area in Botswana. Further north, it can be found in all countries up to Tanzania and over the entire width of the continent.

Description When growing in close proximity to other trees, this evergreen plant is a robust climber, which can reach up to 12 m in height. In open woodland, it can be a small (up to 6 m), bushy, single-stemmed tree with branches down to the ground. It is interesting to note that the genus was named after the two Bauhin brothers, both botanists, who lived in the sixteenth century. Six *Bauhinia* species have tree status in the region. **LEAVES** The butterfly-winged leaves, which are typical of members of *Bauhinia*, are simple and deeply two-lobed. **FLOWERS** Beautiful with their five long (up to 80 mm), crinkly petals; they appear from December-April. **FRUITS** Woody, sharply tipped pods, thickened on one side; they can be up to 300 mm long. When mature, the pods split lengthwise and the two sides spiral. (ZIMBABWE: (Z246) KALAHARI BAUHINIA)

Left: flowers
Above: fruit

Camel's foot (FSA209)   *Piliostigma thonningii*

Kameelspoor

Distribution & habitat The camel's foot covers a large segment of the northern part of the subcontinent, from Swaziland to Limpopo, Mozambique, Zimbabwe, eastern and northern Botswana and the northern extremity of Namibia.

Description It is usually a smallish (up to 6 m, or up to 10 m in the Caprivi Strip), but fairly conspicuous, deciduous tree with a short trunk and a dense, wide-spreading, roundish crown with pendent branches. The bark is pale grey to nearly black and is subdivided into narrow, but not deeply grooved, longitudinal ridges. **LEAVES** Large (up to 120 mm), dark green, glabrous and two-lobed. **FLOWERS** Trumpet-shaped, fairly small and attractive. The crinkly petals are white, sometimes tinged with red at the tips, while the sepals are dark brown due to a dense layer of hairs. Male and female flowers are borne on separate trees (December–February), but look alike. **FRUITS** Unmistakable, undulating pods of up to 220 × 70 mm in size and 15 mm thick. Mature pods are dark brown, woody and indehiscent, but split on the ground.

(ZIMBABWE: (Z249) MONKEYBREAD)

Notes: The soft wood is pale to dark brown. It is not used commercially. Extracts of the pods, seeds and roots are used as dyes and the colours vary from red-brown to dark blue or even black.

Flowers

Fruit

Sjambokpod (FSA212)

Cassia abbreviata subsp. *beareana*

Sambokpeul

Distribution & habitat North of southern Africa, this tropical tree species occurs across the entire width of the continent. In the south, it is found from northeastern Botswana through Zimbabwe to the eastern part of Limpopo and Mpumalanga, southern Mozambique, northern KwaZulu-Natal, Swaziland and in limited areas in northern Namibia.

Description This is a smallish (10 m), deciduous tree with a single stem and a fairly spreading, sometimes roundish, crown. Old bark is dark grey to black and rough. The timber is fairly heavy, hard and dark brown. In frost-free areas, the sjambokpod could be cultivated far more frequently. LEAVES Pinnately compound, with up to 11 pairs of leaflets, which are thin, dull green in colour and marginally entire. FLOWERS Large, dark yellow, measuring 30 mm in diameter and borne in masses at twig terminals; they appear with or just prior to the new leaves in early spring (August–September). The flowering period is quite short (three to four weeks), which is unfortunate as trees in full bloom are a spectacular sight. FRUITS Thin pods that are only 30 mm in diameter, but may be up to about 800 mm long; they remain on the tree for almost a full year. Fruit pulp is dark green and sticky.

(ZIMBABWE: (Z252) SJAMBOKPOD)

Fruit

Flowers

African-wattle (FSA215) *Peltophorum africanum*

Huilboom

Distribution & habitat It has a very wide distribution, occurring over most of northern South Africa (except the eastern Highveld), northern KwaZulu-Natal and Swaziland, southern and northern Botswana, throughout Zimbabwe, most of Mozambique and also in northern Namibia. It is reasonably frost-resistant and therefore also occurs in areas where the temperature can drop below freezing in winter.

Description When not in flower, this tree is inconspicuous; it is one of the smaller African trees and does not possess an outstanding or characteristic configuration. Growing to 10 m, it usually has a short low-branching stem, with the ends of the lower branches near ground level.

LEAVES The leaves are bipinnately compound, feathery, very soft, hairy and reminiscent of the Australian black wattle. **FLOWERS** Bright yellow, relatively large and showy, up to 150 mm long and borne in terminal and axillary sprays. The flowering period is exceptionally long (October–February). The petals are crinkled and the outer sides of the sepals are covered with brown, velvety hairs. **FRUITS** Flat, single-seeded pods with thin, wing-like outer margins; they are borne in dense, hanging clusters.

(ZIMBABWE: (Z257) AFRICAN-WATTLE)

Notes: The heavy, dark brown wood is used to manufacture various commodities. This is one of the most decorative indigenous trees and should feature more extensively in South African gardens.

Left: fruit
Above: flowers

Wild-mango (FSA216)   *Cordyla africana*

Wildemango

Distribution & habitat The wild-mango is found on the eastern side of Africa, from Somalia to KwaZulu-Natal. According to available information, it grows in northeastern KwaZulu-Natal, Swaziland, Mozambique, the Mpumalanga and Limpopo lowveld and southeastern and northern Zimbabwe.

Description It is a large (up to 25 m), deciduous tree with a fairly long, bare stem and a rather dense, wide-spreading crown. One specimen on the Komati River has a spread to about 35 m. Very old bark is dark grey, rough and peels off in thin, irregular sections. The living underbark is dark green.

LEAVES Imparipinnately compound and arranged alternately on the young branches and horizontally placed on either side of the twig, so that the whole resembles a large, bipinnate leaf. Leaflets are thin, up to 45 mm long, light to dark green and shiny. **FLOWERS** Golden-yellow and borne in dense clusters on the basal portion of new twigs, appearing just prior to the new leaves (September–October). Except in colour, they are almost replicas of those of *Schotia brachypetala*, with the stamens being the most important component. **FRUITS** Pods are fleshy, drupaceous, glossy, oval to nearly spherical, up to 80 mm long and golden-yellow when ripe. They drop while still green and ripen on the ground. They contain one or two large seeds embedded in a jelly-like pulp, which is edible and tasty.

(ZIMBABWE: (Z258) WILD-MANGO)

Flowers

Fruit

Keurboom (FSA221)

Virgilia oroboides subsp. *oroboides*

Keurboom

Distribution & habitat The keurboom is endemic to the southwestern and southeastern coastal areas – roughly Cape Town to Port Elizabeth. This tree is one of relatively few pioneer woody species and therefore occupies open areas in or on the edges of evergreen forests and river valleys.

Description Although it also carries the common name 'blossom tree', most English-speaking South Africans probably know it by its Afrikaans name, keurboom. It is fast-growing – it may reach 15 m in height but is usually much smaller – with a short life span. The seeds germinate very easily and, given a suitably moist habitat, seedlings grow up in thousands and may form nearly impenetrable thickets within a few years. Under such conditions, it forms a very slender tree with a long, thin stem and a sparse crown. When growing alone, the crown is upright but fairly wide-spreading and dense. The bark is greyish brown and smooth. At the moment, two species are recognized. *V. divaricata*, which only occurs in the southeastern part of the Western Cape, is much smaller. Its leaves are glossy and dark green; its flowers are dark pink to nearly purple. It is virtually impossible to separate *V. divaricata* from *V. oroboides* in the field. **LEAVES** Pale greyish green, pubescent and imparipinnately compound with between five and 20 pairs of leaflets. **FLOWERS** Pale purple, very attractive and pea-shaped. They are produced in terminal heads in spring and summer. **FRUITS** Pods are velvety and are borne in pendent clusters.

Notes: It is fairly widely used as a garden plant.

Top: flowers
Above: fruit

Tree-wisteria (FSA222)

Bolusanthus speciosus

Vanwykshout

Distribution & habitat According to information available at present, the tree-wisteria extends from northern KwaZulu-Natal to northern Limpopo and eastern Botswana, through the parts of Zimbabwe and into countries north of the Zambezi. It also has a limited distribution in northern and eastern Mozambique. Although it can be found in various soil types, it seems to prefer a high clay content, such as soils derived from dolerite.

Description Usually it is a slender, smallish tree of about 7 m, but it can grow into a much bigger tree with a spreading crown. Stems are fairly straight, often branching low. The bark is brownish grey and longitudinally fissured. Although this tree is deciduous, the leaves are not dropped, or are only partially dropped, if it is watered in winter. **LEAVES** Imparipinnately compound with up to eight pairs of leaflets, plus a terminal leaflet. **FLOWERS** Bluish-mauve and in pendent sprays; if watered, they are partially obscured by the leaves and the trees flower less profusely. Flowers emerge early in spring. **FRUITS** Thin pods are borne in pendent clusters and bulge somewhat over each seed; they turn brown to black when ripe. (ZIMBABWE: (Z263) TREE-WISTERIA)

Notes: The timber resembles that of the wild olive. It is of good quality, fairly heavy and hard. As this is one of the most attractive trees when in full flower (and also one of the relatively few trees from the warmer areas of the subcontinent that can withstand low temperatures), it should be used much more freely in our gardens – with the proviso that it is not watered during the naturally dry period of the year.

Left: flowers
Above: fruit

Sand camwood (FSA223)　　　*Baphia massaiensis* subsp. *obovata*

Sandkamhout

Distribution & habitat This tree is not well known in South Africa, as it occurs only in the northeastern corner of Limpopo, probably only in the Kruger National Park. Further north, in eastern and northern Botswana, western Zimbabwe, the Caprivi Strip and northern Namibia, it is fairly widespread. It grows only in deep, well-drained, sandy soil. The only other member of the genus, *B. racemosa*, is endemic to the KwaZulu-Natal coast.

Description The sand camwood rarely reaches 6 m in height and is usually multi-stemmed. It is deciduous, with a spreading crown only when growing in open woodland. The bark is smooth and dark grey to greyish brown on young stems, becoming longitudinally ridged on old stems.

LEAVES Simple, borne solitarily and fairly far apart. They are obovate, dull green and up to 90 mm long. Two distinct swellings occur on the petiole.

FLOWERS Attractive, pea-like and borne in compact sprays near the ends of the twigs, they are the most outstanding feature of this plant. Petals are pure white (except for a yellow patch at the base of the standard petal), crinkled, very delicate and sweetly scented; sepals are pinkish. They flower in the summer months, but depending on rainfall, may be as late as April.

FRUITS Pods are narrow at the base, broadening towards the tip and ending in a sharp point; they have few seeds. They are hard, shiny and brown when mature and split while on the trees to release their seeds.

(ZIMBABWE: (Z264) SAND CAMWOOD)

Notes: The wood is hard, finely textured and dark brown but, probably due to a lack of large pieces, is not utilized.

Flowers

Broad-leaved fountainbush (FSA226.19) *Psoralea pinnata* var. *latifolia*

Breëblaarfonteinbos

Distribution & habitat This tree has a wide distribution from the eastern parts of the Western Cape, all along the east coast and fairly far inland, up to northern KwaZulu-Natal and possibly southern Mozambique, into the eastern Free State, then north along the Drakensberg escarpment to the Soutpansberg and into the Waterberg region of Limpopo. The common name, fountainbush, aptly describes the habitat of this tree, as it usually grows in wet situations in or near rivers, vleis and marshes. It is seldom abundant. Based on its distribution map, it is justifiable to classify this species as frost-tolerant.

Description The broad-leaved fountainbush is probably deciduous. Full grown specimens can reach as much as 6 m in height and will have a single, bare trunk and a sparse, spreading crown. The bark is smooth and pale brownish grey. Plants in Tsitsikamma are known to have flowered in mid-August, but generally those in the Western Cape flower in October–December, those in the Eastern Cape from February to June and those further north during August–September. Although it is a graceful and attractive tree in its own right, its most prominent assets are its beautiful flowers. **LEAVES** Imparipinnately compound and borne alternately close together at the ends of the slender, soft branches. Leaflets are very fine and slender (sometimes as little as 1 mm wide); they are dark green and shiny. **FLOWERS** Borne in the axils of terminal leaves, they are pea-shaped, light blue to deep blue or even mauve, or rarely, whitish. **FRUITS** Pods are minute, measuring approximately 5 × 3 mm and are enclosed by the persistent calyx.

Top: flowers & fruit
Above: flowers

Corkbush (FSA226)

Mundulea sericea

Kurkbos, Visgif

Distribution & habitat The corkbush grows in northern KwaZulu-Natal, Swaziland, southern Mozambique, all the northern provinces of South Africa (except for the eastern Highveld), the northern and eastern areas of Botswana, northern Namibia and large areas of Zimbabwe. It occurs in a large variety of habitats, but seems to favour sandy soil and a rocky substrate. Judging by its distribution, it should be fairly cold-resistant.

Description It is usually encountered as a multi-stemmed shrub of about 2 m, but can grow into a single-stemmed tree, about 5 m high with a roundish, fairly dense crown. The bark is yellowish grey, very soft and corky, and forms longitudinal ridges, which are easily broken off. **LEAVES** Imparipinnately compound and borne alternately. Leaflets are fairly small (usually about 40 × 15 mm) and are silvery-green due to a layer of silky, silvery hairs. **FLOWERS** Beautiful, pea-like and usually mauve to purple (some in the Pafuri area in the Kruger National Park are white), they are borne in dense sprays at the branch ends (October–January). **FRUITS** Pods are fairly small, borne in pendent clusters and are covered with golden-brown hairs, which later become grey.

(ZIMBABWE: (Z280) CORKBUSH)

Notes: The bark and the seeds contain a chemical substance called rotenone, which is widely used as fish poison. Nevertheless, wild animals will browse the leaves. This is another indigenous tree that should be used more often in gardens.

Flowers

Fruit

Kiaat (FSA236)

Pterocarpus angolensis

Kiaat

Distribution & habitat This is a tropical species with a preference for well-drained soil. It occurs in the northern part of KwaZulu-Natal, Swaziland, the lowveld of Mpumalanga and Limpopo, southern and northern Mozambique, the greater part of Zimbabwe, northern Botswana and the extreme northern area of Namibia.
Description This is a beautiful, single-stemmed, deciduous tree with a wide-spreading, flattened crown. Twice a year these trees are outstandingly noticeable: in autumn, when the leaves are full and dark yellow, and in spring, when flowering. **LEAVES** Large (up to 300 mm long), imparipinnate and pendent. **FLOWERS** Attractive, orange-yellow, emerging immediately prior to, or with, the new leaves. **FRUITS** Pods are exceptional: they can only be recognized as such in the very early stage of development. When mature, they are suborbicular, thickened and spiny in the middle, each surrounded by a thin, but fairly hard, parchment-like wing. They measure up to 100 mm in diameter, are borne in pendent clusters and persist on the trees until the next flowering season.
(**ZIMBABWE:** (Z303) BLOODWOOD, MUKWA; **NAMIBIA:** MUKWA)

Notes: Although the wood is fairly light, it is one of the most favoured furniture woods in the areas of Africa where it occurs. The colour of the heartwood varies from very light brown to red or even copper-brown. It is very durable, easy to work with and polishes well; it is used extensively by African artists to produce sculptures for the curio trade.

Above: flowers
Left: fruit

Kalahari apple-leaf (FSA239)

Philenoptera nelsii

Kalahari-appelblaar

Distribution & habitat In southern Africa, this tropical species occurs only in the northern part of Namibia (including part of the Caprivi Strip), northern Botswana and the western part of Zimbabwe. It grows in various habitats, but seems to thrive in dense or open woodland on Kalahari sand.

Description It often occurs as a multi-stemmed shrub, possibly due to veld fires, but can be a single-stemmed tree up to 10 m high. Small branches often grow from the stem down almost to its base. The crown is usually dense but upright. The bark on young branches is smooth and yellowish grey. It becomes dark grey and peels in thinnish flakes to expose the bark. **LEAVES** Typically imparipinnately compound with one or two pairs and a terminal leaflet, though in Botswana they are usually simple. They are pale green and leathery with prominent net-veining on the underside. The number of leaflets is claimed to increase with higher rainfall – this is not consistent, however, and different variations may occur on the same tree. They are fairly large (up to 120 mm long), velvety when young and glabrous and glossy when old; in autumn they turn bright yellow. **FLOWERS** Pea-shaped flowers are mauve to purple or pinkish and are borne in large (350 mm), terminal sprays. They appear long before the leaves (September–October). **FRUITS** Small, flat, velvety pods that are one-seeded and borne in pendent clusters.

(ZIMBABWE: (Z310) KALAHARI LANCEPOD; NAMIBIA: KALAHARI OMUPANDA)

Notes: The wood is relatively soft, light in weight and pale brown. Although not commonly used – not even as firewood – small household articles are sometimes made from it. The foliage is fairly heavily browsed by game.

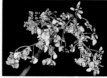
Flowers

Fruit

Wingpod (SA240) — *Xeroderris stuhlmannii*

Vlerkboon

Distribution & habitat In South Africa, this is a very rare tropical tree, as it is restricted to the extreme northeast of Limpopo. In Mozambique and Zimbabwe, however, it is widespread and covers vast areas. In Botswana, it is only known to occur in the eastern and northeastern border regions (Chobe). It also grows in the eastern part of the Caprivi Strip. It seems to prefer well-drained soil.

Description This deciduous tree has a single tall stem and a spreading, fairly dense crown. It usually reaches a height of 10 m, though may be taller. The wood is pale to dark yellow, finely textured and finishes smoothly. On old stems, bark is grey and peels off in small, flat, irregular blocks. When damaged, the bark exudes a blood-red cell sap, which is used as a dye. **LEAVES** Shed late in winter, they are large (reaching nearly 400 mm in length) and imparipinnately compound. Leaflets are big (up to 80 mm long) and dark green. **FLOWERS** Small, pea-like, white, waxy and borne in fairly sparse racemes at the bases of new twigs (September–December). **FRUITS** Clusters of pendent pods that are oblong, up to 300 mm long and flat. The central portion is thickened, prominently veined and hard; the outside is a membranous wing. Pods are brown at maturity and fall while still unopened. Young pods are sometimes damaged by insects: they then develop into deformed, spherical 'fruits' resembling berries.
(ZIMBABWE: (Z313) WINGPOD; NAMIBIA: WINGBEAN)

Notes: Leaves are browsed by game and domestic stock, though they are possibly poisonous. This tree is the host of a very rare species of mistletoe, *Vanwykia remota*, which, in southern Africa, has only been found in the northern Kruger National Park.

Far left: flowers
Left: fruit

Nyalatree (FSA241)   *Xanthocercis zambesiaca*

Njalaboom

Distribution & habitat The nyalatree has an easterly distribution in Africa, reaching as far south as the Mpumalanga lowveld. It also occurs in northern and northwestern Limpopo, eastern Botswana and the southern and northwestern areas of Zimbabwe and Mozambique.

Description This tree is evergreen to semi-deciduous. It usually has a single, short trunk. Old stems are grooved and dented; branch-ends are pendent. Bark is grey and rough but does not peel off. The official dimensions of one particularly large nyalatree are: height 22 m; spread 29.8 m; girth 11.2 m, although the spread of a tree on the bank of the Limpopo River (Tuli Block, Botswana) was 55 m. There may be even larger ones, as these are huge, impressive trees. **LEAVES** Imparipinnately compound; leaflets are a shiny dark green. **FLOWERS** Small, white, borne in short, axillary or terminal sprays and sweetly scented (November–December). **FRUITS** Initially pod-shaped, but develop into oval or ovoid drupes (berries) up to 25 mm in length. They become yellow-green to yellow-brown at maturity. Fruit pulp is floury, sticky and edible.

(ZIMBABWE: (Z314) NYALATREE)

Notes: While still on the trees, the fruit is eaten by a variety of birds, as well as primates. These animals also dislodge fruits, which are then eaten by nyala, bushbuck, impala and other animals; browsers also consume the leaves.

Flowers

Fruit & seeds

BRAAM VAN WYK

Coraltree (FSA245)

Erythrina lysistemon

Koraalboom

Distribution & habitat Of the seven tree species of *Erythrina* on the sub-continent, this one has the widest natural distribution, occurring from the Eastern Cape through KwaZulu-Natal, Swaziland and southern Mozambique to Mpumalanga, Gauteng, the North West province, Limpopo and Botswana. In Zimbabwe, it has been recorded in the southwestern, central and eastern areas.

Description The common coraltree may be propagated by means of seeds and cuttings: even big branches take root easily. The tree is not very particular with regard to habitat and can therefore be grown successfully in just about all soil types and rainfall regimes. **LEAVES** Trifoliolate, and characterized by small hooked thorns on the underside of the petiole and main veins. These thorns are also scattered along the branches. The small, hard, whitish green galls, which occur in the leaves, are caused by insects and, while they are not detrimental, they are unsightly. **FLOWERS** Brilliantly red and densely packed in terminal heads, they emerge in spring long before the leaves. If trees are watered in winter, old leaves are only partially discarded and flowers do not show up as well as on bare trees. They also seem to flower less profusely. **FRUITS** Cylindrical, black pods that are constricted between the seeds.
(ZIMBABWE: (Z318) SACRED CORALTREE)

Flowers

Fruit

Small greenthorn (FSA252) *Balanites pedicellaris* subsp. *pedicellaris*

Kleingroendoring

Distribution & habitat Although this is a widespread, tropical species, it occupies only a relatively small area in southern Africa, extending from the southeastern corner of Botswana (Tuli Block) eastwards in a narrow belt on either side of the Limpopo River, into Mozambique and then southwards (also through Mpumalanga) to northeastern KwaZulu-Natal. Small greenthorn is relatively abundant in northeastern KwaZulu-Natal (at least in the Ndumu Game Reserve). It is found on poorly-drained, clayey soil, where it is a component of the nearly impenetrable thornbush thickets. The only time this tree is really conspicuous is when bearing fruit, which is sometimes borne in masses.

Description It is usually an untidy shrub, sometimes with long shoots, found in dense bush. However, it may attain a height of 6 m in open conditions. It is then single-stemmed and upright, with a spreading, very sparse crown. The bark splits into small, boat-shaped sections. Even young twigs are exceptionally hard and may vary in colour from buff-green to yellowish brown. Old stems are deeply dented and fluted, similar to those of *B. maughamii*. It is armed with single, straight, long, sharp and hairy spines. **LEAVES** Compound with two velvety leaflets that are markedly brownish and pubescent when young. **FLOWERS** Yellowish green, inconspicuous and borne in groups of three in leaf-axils; present from spring to summer, depending on rainfall. **FRUITS** They are about 25 mm in diameter and consist of a single, hard stone covered with a thin, fleshy layer, which is edible but not tasty; an attractive deep orange colour when ripe.

(ZIMBABWE: (Z327) SMALL TORCHWOOD)

Fruit

Flowers

Cape-chestnut (FSA256)

Calodendrum capense

Kaapse kastaiing

Distribution & habitat When in flower, this is one of the most beautiful trees in southern Africa. It is a forest species, occurring all along the east coast of South Africa roughly from Mossel Bay to northern KwaZulu-Natal and along the escarpment of Swaziland to the Soutpansberg. In Zimbabwe, it mainly grows in the eastern forests, where it also enters Mozambique. They are highly visible on the Western Cape's Garden Route during their flowering period (October–December), especially when taking the old road through the Grootrivier and Bloukrans passes.

Description Although usually a smallish tree, it can reach 20 m in favourable conditions. It is single-stemmed, often branching fairly low down the trunk, and has a dense crown, which spreads in open conditions only. The bark is grey and smooth. Although evergreen, it may lose its leaves in dry conditions. **LEAVES** Simple, rather big (up to 120 × 70 mm) and occur in opposite pairs. They are aromatic and characterized by scattered, translucent gland-dots. **FLOWERS** Petals are mostly pink, sometimes nearly white, and the five sterile stamens are always pink with maroon to purple gland-dots. They are striking and remain attractive for several weeks. **FRUITS** Five-lobed, woody capsules, about 40 mm in diameter, covered with small wart-like knobs. **(ZIMBABWE: (Z336) CAPE-CHESTNUT)**

Left: ripe fruit
Above: flowers

White-ironwood (FSA261)

Vepris lanceolata

Witysterhout

Distribution & habitat The white-ironwood occurs all along the coast, as well as fairly deep inland, from the Western Cape to northern KwaZulu-Natal and from the Mozambique coast as far as Beira. In the northern parts of South Africa, it is confined to the mountainous regions from the Magaliesberg to the Soutpansberg. It grows mostly in dry shrub forest and in dense thickets on coastal dunes.

Description White-ironwood may reach a height of 20 m when growing in evergreen forest. Under favourable conditions, the crown of this evergreen tree may be fairly wide-spreading with a long and straight trunk. Bark is smooth grey to pale brown with orange and white blotches. **LEAVES** Trifoliolate; leaflets are hard, dull green, markedly wavy, gland-dotted and lemon-scented. **FLOWERS** Very small, yellowish and borne in fairly large, terminal sprays (December–March, depending on rainfall). **FRUITS** Small, roughly spherical and segmented, they are borne in dense clusters; they turn from purple to black at maturity (autumn to spring).

Notes: The wood is white, very hard, strong and even-grained, and has been used for numerous purposes.

Top: *flowers*
Above: *fruit*

Mountain seringa (FSA269)

Kirkia wilmsii

Bergsering

Distribution & habitat The mountain seringa is locally abundant, but its distribution is limited to South Africa, occupying a horseshoe-shaped area from the southern lowveld of Mpumalanga northwards to the Soutpansberg and then southwards, stopping short of Pretoria and Rustenburg. It only occurs on mountains.

Description This is a deciduous tree, which is striking and noticeable in its spring apparel of pale green, as well as its dark reddish brown to yellow of autumn. It is usually either multi-stemmed or low branching. The crowns of old trees have a fairly wide spread and the branches are often on the ground. Young trees are slender and upright. The bark is dark grey and smooth with irregular sections of dead bark. LEAVES Borne close together at the ends of the branches, they are imparipinnately compound with a large number of leaflets, creating a feathery appearance. Leaflet margins are inconspicuously, but coarsely, serrate. FLOWERS Small, white and borne in axillary panicles with long, slender stalks (September–October). FRUITS Small, capsule-like and borne in fairly large clusters. They are roughly oblong (up to 11 × 6 mm) and composed of four joined triangular parts, with joints showing as sharp ridges. When mature, they split along ridges and often persist on the tree until the next flowering season.

Notes: The timber is dirty white to pale brown and fairly light and soft, yet has a fine texture. It works easily, but is apparently not worth much. It has been reported that the tree is browsed by game and domestic stock.

BRAAM VAN WYK

Left: bark
Top: flowers
Above: fruit

Paperbark corkwood (FSA278)

Commiphora marlothii

Papierbaskanniedood

Distribution & habitat The paperbark corkwood occurs in central and northern Limpopo, eastern Botswana, various areas in Zimbabwe and in Mozambique. It is almost always found in rocky situations.

Description It has a single, bare trunk and a spreading, not particularly dense, crown; the stem is very characteristic. The dirty-white to yellow bark peels off in large, thin, papery strips and flakes – even on young branches. Exposed, living bark is bright yellow-green. It is deciduous.

LEAVES Imparipinnately compound and borne at the tips of the branches; they may be up to 200 mm long.

Leaflets are fairly large (80 × 40 mm), pale green and distinctly hairy; margins are largely crenate. **FLOWERS** Small, yellow-green and borne in very small, dense inflorescences on long, hairy stems (September–October, depending on rain). **FRUITS** Roughly oblong, borne in tight, pendent clusters on long, hairy stalks. They are symmetrical and longitudinally subdivided by a distinct groove; they turn pale red when ripening. Seeds (stones) persist on the tree after the flesh has fallen and the red pseudo-aril at their base covers only a small portion of the stone, extending into four thin, smooth 'fingers'.
(ZIMBABWE: (Z357) PAPERBARK CORKWOOD)

Notes: The timber is pale brown, soft and worthless.

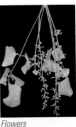

Flowers

Bark

Fruit

Pepper-leaved corkwood (FSA281)   *Commiphora mossambicensis*

Peperblaarkanniedood

Distribution & habitat This species stops just short of the northern South African border, but covers most of the Zimbabwean territory, the north and east of Botswana, the Caprivi Strip and the northern tip of Mozambique (after which it has been named).

Description It may reach 10 m in height, but is usually not more than about 6 m. It is single-stemmed with a sparsely branched, spreading crown. Young twigs are reddish brown. Young sideshoots are often exceptionally thick at the base. The bark is brown or reddish grey and smooth. These trees are most noticeable during autumn (April–May), when the leaves turn bright yellow before dropping. **LEAVES** Characteristic, either trifoliolate, with two pairs and a terminal leaflet, or with one pair plus a solitary leaflet and a terminal leaflet. The leaflets are exceptionally large, ovate to almost circular (up to 80 × 80 mm) and bright pale green. The margins, especially in young leaves, are hair-fringed. Leaves have a peppery smell. **FLOWERS** Small, yellowish and borne in axillary groups (October– December). **FRUITS** Almost spherical, they are about 10 mm in diameter and turn reddish when mature. Seeds are black with a prominent, bright red pseudo-aril that has 'fingers' that nearly reach the top of the seed. The roundish fruits sometimes take almost a full year to reach maturity. (ZIMBABWE: (Z359) PEPPER-LEAVED CORKWOOD)

Notes: The wood is used to make small household articles, but is soft and not worth much.

Fruit

Fruit

Flowers

Mountain mahogany (FSA293)

Entandrophragma caudatum

Bergmahonie

Distribution & habitat This is a tropical species, extending southwards into Mozambique, Zimbabwe (widespread), northeastern Botswana, the northern and northeastern areas of Limpopo, eastern parts of Mpumalanga, northern KwaZulu-Natal and Swaziland.

Description This deciduous tree is very conspicuous when in its full autumn dress of bright yellow leaves. It can reach a height of 30 m and has a long, thickset, straight trunk and a very wide-spreading crown. The bark pattern is similar to that of the marula (*Sclerocarya birrea* subsp. *caffra*).

LEAVES Paripinnately compound, up to nearly 300 mm long and closely packed at twig terminals. **FLOWERS** Inconspicuous, greenish yellow and borne immediately below or in the axils of new leaves (September). **FRUITS** In contrast to flowers, fruits are large and very conspicuous, especially when ripe (up to 220 mm long). They are pendent, cudgel-shaped, hard and woody, turning from an initial shiny-green to purplish brown and then dark brown. At maturity, pericarps split into five backward-curving valves, revealing the central column with neatly embedded winged seeds – they resemble a peeled banana at this stage. (ZIMBABWE: (Z369) WOODEN-BANANA; NAMIBIA: CAPRIVI WOODEN-BANANA)

Notes: The wood is fairly hard, heavy and dark reddish brown. It is valued as a furniture wood. Palgrave (2005) states that it was the royal tree of Barotseland in Zambia, and that barges were made from it for the Paramount Chiefs.

Top: fruit
Above: flowers

Cape-ash (FSA298)

Ekebergia capensis

Essenhout

Distribution & habitat The Cape-ash is widespread along the east coast from the Cape Peninsula to northern KwaZulu-Natal, in the Mpumalanga lowveld, Limpopo, Mozambique and eastern Zimbabwe. An isolated population also occurs in northern Botswana. It is a tropical species that occurs as far north as Ethiopia and Sudan.

Description It is a single-stemmed, evergreen tree with a dense, spreading crown; it can be up to 20 m in height. The ends of its branches are pendent and are often as low as ground level. Stems are usually rather short and the bark is dented, grooved, dark grey and slightly rough. This is one of the fastest growing indigenous trees; seeds should be planted fresh.

LEAVES Large (up to 300 mm long), imparipinnately compound, usually with five pairs and a terminal leaflet, and borne at the ends of the twigs. Leaflets are symmetrical, between 50 and 95 mm long, glabrous, moderately hard, shiny and dark green. **FLOWERS** Very small, white and borne in long (up to 170 mm), sparse, branched racemes just below or in axils of older leaves (October–November). **FRUITS** Roughly spherical, up to 20 mm in diameter, and attractively bright red when ripe. A thin, soft exocarp (outer layer) encloses a white, slightly sticky, soft fruit pulp, which contains two to four seeds.

(ZIMBABWE: (Z377) DOGPLUM)

Notes: The timber is off-white to pale brown with a reddish tinge. It is finely textured, fairly light, quite soft and not durable. A variety of wild animals eat the fruit.

Left: fruit & seeds
Above: flowers

Bushveld Natal-mahogany (FSA301)   *Trichilia emetica* subsp. *emetica*

Bosveldrooiessenhout

Distribution & habitat This tropical species occurs from KwaZulu-Natal to the northern areas of Zimbabwe and Mozambique. It also features in the area around Kazangula, where Namibia, Botswana and Zimbabwe meet. It grows near water or in high-rainfall areas.

Description Bushveld Natal-mahogany is a fairly large (up to 20 m), attractive tree with a short, often dented, trunk and a very dense and wide-spreading crown. Branch-ends are usually pendent and may reach ground level. The bark is grey-brown and usually smooth. **LEAVES** Imparipinnately compound and may be as much as 500 mm long. Leaflets are up to 160 × 55 mm (though they are usually about half that size) and are borne quite far apart; they are elliptic to oblong-elliptic, glabrous, glossy, very dark green above and dull green with pale brown pubescence below. **FLOWERS** Small, tubiform, predominantly green and borne in large, dense racemes near the twig terminals (September–October). **FRUITS** Female trees always bear lots of fruit, while male trees never do. Fruits are pubescent, pale buff-green, roughly pear-shaped and longitudinally segmented in three capsules. They dehisce while on the tree to expose the attractive seeds, which are nearly totally enclosed by orange-coloured arils. The small, oval portion (which is not covered) is pitch-black.

(ZIMBABWE: (Z380) NATAL-MAHOGANY)

Centre: flowers
Left: fruit
Above: bark

Violet-tree (FSA303)

Securidaca longepedunculata

Krinkhout

Distribution & habitat In South Africa, this tropical species extends southwards, nearing Pretoria and Rustenburg. It is also widespread in Zimbabwe and Mozambique, parts of Botswana and the northern region of Namibia. It occurs in woodland, probably always in sandy soil, but is not abundant in any region.

Description The violet-tree is a single-stemmed, deciduous tree with a dense, twiggy, but poorly spreading crown; the trunk is often shallowly fluted. The bark is largely smooth and very pale grey. The largest specimen on which information has been published by the Dendrological Society grows near Makopane in Limpopo. It is 9 m high with a spread of 10.6 m and a trunk diameter of 950 mm. **LEAVES** Fairly small and grouped together on short lateral shoots. **FLOWERS** Beautiful flowers are produced in such profusion (September–November) that trees will be completely covered, given ideal climatic conditions. Reminiscent of legume flowers in structure, they vary in colour from pink to mauve. **FRUITS** Very characteristic, consisting of roughly oval, hard, fairly small nuts with large (up to 40 mm), membranous, hatchet-shaped wings. They are purplish green when young and light brown when mature. They remain on the tree for about a year. **(ZIMBABWE: (Z383)** VIOLET-TREE)

Notes: Locals use the fleshy roots of this plant, medicinally and otherwise. Oil extracted from the roots contains 99% pure methyl salicylate; it has a pungent smell, exactly like that of household remedies for stiff or strained muscles.

Female flowers

Fruit

Feverberry (FSA329)   *Croton megalobotrys*

Koorsbessie

Distribution & habitat This species is common in the Mpumalanga and Limpopo lowveld and adjacent areas, but less so in the North West province and adjoining Botswana; however, it is very prominent in the north of Botswana, as well as the northwestern and northern parts of Zimbabwe. It also features in central and northeastern Zimbabwe and large areas of Mozambique.

Description It is deciduous or semi-deciduous and has been reported at a height of 20 m, but it is usually less than half that size. It has a single, fairly short trunk and a spreading, leafy and exceptionally dense crown. The stem is usually low-branching, bent, grooved and fairly smooth. The bark is grey-brown with a yellowish tinge; it has a thin outer layer of dead bark, which splits into longitudinal strips. **LEAVES** Simple, fairly large, cordate (heart-shaped), very thin and smooth above but rough beneath (they are usually about 70 × 55 mm, but sometimes up to 180 × 145 mm). Young leaves have stellate (star-shaped) hairs on both surfaces. The margins are irregularly serrate. **FLOWERS** Inconspicuous, yellowish green and axillary, they are borne in long, sparse, spicate racemes (up to 110 mm long) at the ends of the twigs (October–November). Male and female flowers occur in the same raceme, with female florets at the base. **FRUITS** Roughly pear-shaped, trilocular and about 35 mm in length, they become brownish yellow when ripe (February–March).

(ZIMBABWE: (Z391) FEVERBERRY)

BRAAM VAN WYK

Left: nuts
Top: flowers
Above: fruit

Manketti (FSA337)

Schinziophyton rautanenii

Manketti

Distribution & habitat This tree (previously *Ricinodendron rautanenii*) occupies a wide strip on either side of the Botswana/Zimbabwe border as far as Kasane, and then spreads west through northern Botswana and northern Namibia. From Kasane, it extends eastwards for some distance and then stops. In South Africa, it occurs only in northwestern Limpopo near the border with Botswana. Beautiful specimens can be seen on the road between the Ngoma bridge and Katima Mulilo in the Caprivi Strip. This species prefers a well-drained habitat, such as Kalahari sand, and often forms pure stands.

Description The manketti is one of the larger African trees (up to 20 m). It is deciduous and has a single, long, very thickset trunk and a wide-spreading crown. The tree in the photograph is 15 m high and the stem has a girth of 4 m. **LEAVES** Hairy and digitately compound with five to seven largish leaflets (up to 110 × 50 mm); petioles are long (150 mm). **FLOWERS** Yellow and about 10 mm in diameter; each sex is on a separate tree (October–November). **FRUITS** Slightly oval, about 30 mm long and grey-green, as a result of the velvety hairs covering them; they are yellowish when ripe. The pulp, which is only a few millimetres thick, covers a large kernel. It is woody and difficult to crack. The seed is edible and contains yellow oil.

(ZIMBABWE: (Z419) MANKETTITREE; NAMIBIA: MANKETTI)

Top: flowers
Above: fruit

Naboom (FSA351)

Euphorbia ingens

Naboom

Distribution & habitat This species grows mostly in countries on the eastern side of Africa. In the Eastern Cape, Swaziland, KwaZulu-Natal and Mpumalanga, it is found only to the east of the escarpment. From Limpopo, its range extends westwards to include eastern Botswana and southwest to include the Magaliesberg (North West province). In Zimbabwe, it occurs in the southern, western, central and northern areas, extending into Mozambique.

Description The species name *ingens* means 'large, massive or enormous', aptly describing the tree, which can reach roughly 12 m. Its stem is short and the massive crown is very dense. The bark is grey to dark grey, slightly rough and dented. Branches are usually four-sided with four ridges (sometimes five or six). They branch freely and are conspicuously articulated with about 100 mm in diameter between opposite ridges. If the green outer layer is pierced, latex will stream from the wound. **FLOWERS** Floral buds are situated close to the spines and develop into groups of three yellow-green flowers on a common peduncle about 10 mm in length (May–June). **FRUITS** Mature fruits are green, nearly spherical, up to 13 mm in diameter and dehisce, while on the tree, to release seeds. Usually only one fruit develops from a group of flowers.
(ZIMBABWE: (Z437) GIANT EUPHORBIA)

Notes: The timber is fibrous, soft and useless.

Left: flowers: male (centre), female (left & right)
Above: fruit

Marula (FSA360)

Sclerocarya birrea subsp. *caffra*

Maroela

Distribution & habitat The marula is widespread from KwaZulu-Natal through Swaziland and into South Africa's northern provinces, Mozambique, Zimbabwe, large areas of Botswana and the northern areas of Namibia.
Description It is a deciduous, single-stemmed tree with a wide-spreading crown. **LEAVES** Imparipinnately compound, up to 300 mm long and crowded at the ends of the twigs. **FLOWERS** Small and rather inconspicuous; the two sexes occur on separate trees. Flowering starts in August–September and the berries usually ripen in January–February. **FRUITS** The marula's biggest asset; fruits are fairly large, yellow berries with a nauseatingly sweet smell. The seeds taste like walnuts and contain about 50% oil, which is rich in protein.
(ZIMBABWE: (Z483) MARULA)

Notes: The bark contains a substance similar to antihistamine and has been successfully used in the treatment of blisters caused by hairy caterpillars. Water can be obtained from the roots. The timber is tough and can be used for various purposes. Leaves are consumed by a variety of game. The white, slimy fruit pulp is rich in vitamin C and can be eaten as is or made into a refreshing drink, a potent alcoholic beverage, an excellent conserve and the well-known pale yellow to reddish jelly.

Left: fruit
Above: flowers

Wildplum (FSA361)

Harpephyllum caffrum

Wildepruim

Distribution & habitat This is almost exclusively a South African tree, occurring from the Eastern Cape to northern KwaZulu-Natal, the southernmost area of Mozambique, Swaziland and then along the escarpment to the Soutpansberg. It is the only representative of the genus. It is often found in moist situations, but also grows on rocky hillsides in the Eastern Cape.

Description The wildplum is evergreen, single-stemmed and has a dense, wide-spreading crown. The stem branches fairly low and branch ends are sometimes pendent. It may reach 15 m, but is normally much smaller. Its bark is dark brown and rough. Although not related, this tree looks much like some forms of the Cape-ash. The major difference is the symmetry/asymmetry of the leaflets. The fruit can be used to produce wine and jelly. Birds and primates relish the fruit. **LEAVES** Crowded at the twig terminals, they are imparipinnately compound with four to eight pairs of leaflets, plus a terminal leaflet. Leaflets are slightly sickle-shaped, asymmetric, glossy and dark green. The oldest leaves are shed continuously and turn red before dropping. **FLOWERS** Small, white and borne in axillary sprays; each sex is on a separate tree. **FRUITS** Oval, up to 20 mm long and red when ripe. They are edible, but sour, and the pulp is rather thin.

Notes: The wood is reddish, rather heavy and finishes well. It has been used for manufacturing furniture and other commodities. The wildplum has been planted extensively in both South Africa and Zimbabwe, often as street trees; young plants are sold at some nurseries.

Flowers

Fruit   Fruit

BRAAM VAN WYK

Red-beech (FSA364)   *Protorhus longifolia*

Rooiboekenhout

Distribution & habitat Only its presence in Swaziland robs this species of South African endemism status. It occurs in forests and open woodland, sometimes on rocky hillsides, all along the coast from the Eastern Cape to northern KwaZulu-Natal, where it deviates inland and follows the escarpment to the Soutpansberg.

Description Red-beech is an evergreen tree with a fairly long, bare trunk and bare branches. The bark is rather smooth, grey and mottled on young branches; it cracks lengthwise with age. It exudes a sticky gum. This tree may reach 15 m in height.

The crown is wide-spreading. **LEAVES** Simple, crowded near the branch tips and borne opposite or subopposite. They are narrowly-elliptic, up to 150 mm long, hard, dark green and glossy with prominent veins, especially on the undersurface. Old leaves turn yellow to bright red before being shed. **FLOWERS** Although the yellowish green flowers are very small, they are borne in fairly large, dense, conspicuous, axillary clusters at the twig terminals, with the two sexes on separate trees. The flowering period is from August to October. **FRUITS** Fleshy, asymmetric, about 10 mm in diameter and glossy; they turn purple when ripening (October–December).

Notes: The timber is of fairly good quality but is not durable.

Fruit

Female flowers

Male flowers

Tarwood (FSA365)

Loxostylis alata

Teerhout

Distribution & habitat Tarwood is endemic to South Africa, occurring in the Eastern Cape and KwaZulu-Natal. Specimens can be seen in the Suurberg National Park, as well as in the Oribi Gorge Nature Reserve. This species seems to prefer a fairly well-drained soil, as it is often found on rocky hillsides and outcrops, though it also grows along riverbanks.

Description This evergreen tree usually has a short, single stem and a wide-spreading, roundish and very dense crown. The bark is grey to dark grey, fairly rough and forms narrow, longitudinal ridges, which sometimes crack crosswise to form small blocks. It can be up to 10 m high. Flowering usually starts in September–October

but may be as late as the following autumn; because of the persistent, colourful sepals, the female trees look spectacular for months on end. **LEAVES** Characteristic: imparipinnately compound with up to five pairs of leaflets and a distinctly winged rachis. Old leaves are dull green to yellowish green, while young leaves are often attractively tinged with red. **FLOWERS** Smallish, white, star-shaped and borne in large, branched, terminal panicles, with each sex on a separate tree. The persistent sepals are the most conspicuous part of the flower. They are petal-like and become pink to red and eventually straw-coloured when the fruit ripens. **FRUITS** Small and fleshy, they are situated at the base in the middle of the star-shaped 'flower' formed by the sepals.

Flowers

Fruit

Resintree (FSA375)

Ozoroa paniculosa subsp. *paniculosa*

Harpuisboom

Distribution & habitat This species can be found in most of the bushveld areas of KwaZulu-Natal, Gauteng, Mpumalanga, Limpopo, the North West province, southern Mozambique, southern Zimbabwe and large parts of Botswana, as well as northern and southern Namibia. It prefers well-drained substrates and is therefore found most frequently on sandy soil or hillsides.

Description This is a deciduous tree that loses its leaves late in spring. It is normally smallish (9 m) with a short trunk and a poorly spreading crown. The bark is pale to dark grey and breaks up into small blocks. Suckers often sprout from the base of the stem. The milky sap is sticky and smells like resin. LEAVES Simple and generally borne in verticils of three, they are oblong/oval, up to 170 mm long (mostly smaller), dark green above and silvery and tomentose (downy) underneath; margins are minutely crenate (scalloped). The most notable characteristic is the herringbone pattern formed by the main and secondary veins, which is the common feature linking the *Ozoroa* species. FLOWERS Small, white and borne in terminal clusters during mid-summer. FRUITS Kidney-shaped, initially shiny and bright green with reddish brown spots, turning to reddish brown (sunny side); at maturity, they turn black and raisin-like. (ZIMBABWE: (Z491) RESINTREE; NAMIBIA: COMMON RESINBUSH)

Notes: The wood does not burn readily, probably on account of the resin, and partially burnt logs are a common sight after veld fires.

Top: flowers
Above: fruit

Red crowberry (FSA380)

Searsia chirindensis

Bostaaibos

Distribution & habitat This deciduous tree occurs in evergreen forests along the east coast from the southwestern Cape to southern Mozambique. From northern KwaZulu-Natal, it follows the escarpment to the Soutpansberg and into Zimbabwe as far as Mutare in the east, where it also crosses into the forests on the Chimanimani Mountains of Mozambique.

Description It is by far the largest of the *Searsia* trees. Although large trees are common in the Tsitsikamma/Knysna forests, outside these forests it is a smallish shrub with short, spiny-tipped lateral branchlets. Large specimens have fairly long trunks with a dense and wide-spreading crown. The bark changes from smooth and pale grey-brown to dark brown and rough with longitudinal cracks. **LEAVES** Trifoliolate leaves, like those of all other *Searsia* species. Leaflets are large (up to 120 mm long) with a very long petiole, tapering into a long, prominent tip. The midrib is yellowish, but is often tinged with red. **FLOWERS** Exceptionally small, yellowish green and borne in large axillary and terminal heads (October–March). **FRUITS** They are small, round, flat and turn red when ripe. Mature, unripe fruit has been found in August (in Knysna) and nearly-mature fruit in January (in the Pretoria National Botanical Garden).

(ZIMBABWE: (Z494) RED CURRANT CROWBERRY)

Left: fruit
Above: flowers

Karee (FSA386)

Searsia lancea

Karee

Distribution & habitat Occurs in a belt, varying tremendously in width, from northern Namibia, southwards to the Western Cape and then northwards through the Karoo, the Free State, Gauteng, the North West province and the western half of Limpopo into Zimbabwe and eastern Botswana. It can be found in a variety of habitats, but is usually prominent in low-lying areas near watercourses.

Description It generally grows to about 8 m in height, with a short stem, a dense, rather roundish crown and trailing branchlets. The bark is dark grey and rough. As this species is one of the relatively few frost-tolerant evergreen trees on the subcontinent, it is very widely cultivated and is one of the few indigenous trees widely propagated by nurseries. **LEAVES** Trifoliolate, as with all *Searsia* species. They are dark green, shiny, narrow and long, with entire margins. **FLOWERS** Very small, greenish, sweetly scented and borne in large, dense, pendent clusters at the twig terminals; each sex is on a different tree (June–September). **FRUITS** Small and almost spherical, they are shiny and brown when ripe.
(ZIMBABWE: (Z497) WILLOW CROWBERRY; NAMIBIA: KAREE)

Notes: The wood is finely textured, reddish brown, hard, tough and durable. In areas where frost is a problem, the karee should be used to supply necessary shade.

Left: young stem
Top: flowers
Above: fruit

Common saffronwood (FSA415) — *Elaeodendron croceum*

Gewone saffraan

Distribution & habitat The common saffronwood is mainly a South African species, following the east coast from the Cape Peninsula to KwaZulu-Natal and along the escarpment, through Swaziland and into Mpumalanga as far as the Soutpansberg in Limpopo. It then vanishes, only to reappear in the 'tree-paradise' on the eastern border of Zimbabwe. It grows from sea-level to rather far inland, at forest margins, in wooded ravines and in valleys.

Description It is an evergreen tree with a short trunk, low branches and a dense-spreading, drooping crown. The grey-brown bark is smooth and thin with orange underbark and small cracks. This tree frequently occurs in shrub form, but may attain a height of about 10 m (in ideal conditions). **LEAVES** Simple leaves borne in opposite or sub-opposite pairs, they are medium-large (usually about 60 × 30 mm), leathery, thick, dark green and glossy. Margins are hardened with sharp-tipped, widely-spaced teeth. **FLOWERS** Inconspicuous, small, greenish white and borne in small, compact heads at twig terminals (August–March). **FRUITS** Ovoid and white to pale lemon-yellow, up to 25 mm long and often covered with wrinkles or encrustations. They reach maturity during the following flowering season.

(ZIMBABWE: (Z523) FOREST-SAFFRON)

Notes: Information on the timber is lacking.

82

BRAAM VAN WYK

Left: fruit
Above: flowers

Bittersweet-cherry (FSA417)

Maurocenia frangula

Nastergalkersie

Distribution & habitat It is known that many plants have clear-cut preferences with regard to ecological factors, such as day length, soil conditions, moisture availability, shelter from wind, maximum and minimum temperatures, sun or shade, etc. Some of these plants are extremely sensitive to certain conditions and will only grow in very confined areas. The bittersweet-cherry is apparently one of these: it is found only in a restricted area in the Western Cape. The tree pictured above is one of a very small population in the West Coast National Park growing on wind-blown sand on the exposed summit of Postberg hill. It apparently also occurs in coastal bush and along mountain streams.

Description The bittersweet-cherry is an evergreen tree growing to approximately 5 m in height, usually having a short, single trunk and a slightly spreading, very dense crown. The grey bark is somewhat rough and scaly, peeling off in flat flakes. **LEAVES** Young leaves have extremely attractive colouring: being dark red to nearly purple. They are borne in opposite pairs and are simple, almost circular in shape and very dark green, becoming thick, leathery and hard when old. **FLOWERS** Whitish, very small and borne axillary near the tips of branches. Flowering occurs from May to June. **FRUITS** Two-seeded, slightly oval in shape and occur in small bunches; they are fairly small (15 mm) and have an attractive red colour when ripe (August).

Notes: The timber is yellow, fine-grained, hard and tough. It has been used to make musical instruments.

Flowers

Fruit & seed

Jacketplum (FSA433)   *Pappea capensis*

Doppruim

Distribution & habitat This species is common in the arid southern part of Namibia and the Northern Cape. It is the dominant tree in large areas of the Eastern Cape; from there it extends northwards into Mozambique, most of northern South Africa and Zimbabwe and into eastern Botswana.

Description Over most of its range, the jacketplum is a small tree (7 m), but may reach a height of 12 m. It is deciduous with a short trunk and a fairly dense, spreading crown. The wood has a fine grain and is quite heavy, hard and pale brown with a reddish tinge. The Zimbabwean name 'indaba tree' stems from the fact that Lobengula, a chief of the Matabele, held meetings (indabas) with his headmen in the shade of one of these trees. **LEAVES** Usually crowded at the ends of the branches, they are simple, variable in size, hard and rough; margins may be entire or finely spine-toothed. **FLOWERS** Borne in long spikes; they are male at first and later female. **FRUITS** An outstanding characteristic feature of this tree is its fruit – they are soft, hairy, green, round berries, which are up to about 15 mm in diameter. During some seasons, the berries occur in masses. At ripening, pericarps split in two to reveal a bright red, fleshy, shining false-aril, which envelops the black seed.

(ZIMBABWE: (Z554) INDABATREE; NAMIBIA: JACKETPLUM)

Notes: The fleshy part of the fruit is delicious and is enjoyed by both people and animals. It is also used to make jelly and to brew an alcoholic beverage. The quality of the wood is good enough for a variety of purposes, but large pieces are rare.

Left: flowers & fruit
Above: flowers

Cape hemp (FSA457)

Sparrmannia africana

Kaapse stokroos

Distribution & habitat It is endemic to the southeastern and eastern coastal regions of the Western Cape and the Eastern Cape. Palgrave (2005) refers to the Cape hemp as a 'rampant weed at the margins of evergreen forest'; this characteristic is well-illustrated along the Garden Route in the Tsitsikamma area, where some plants became established on the verge of a road that had been cleared during construction.

Description As this evergreen plant is seen most frequently as a multi-stemmed shrub 2–3 m in height, its inclusion in a tree list may be criticized. However, in a suitable habitat, it may reach a height of 7 m. Its growth-habit is shrub-like, with some branches at ground level. Its bark is smooth, even shiny, and greyish brown. **LEAVES** Simple, large (up to 150 mm long), heart-shaped, three- to nine-veined from the base, soft and prominently hairy. They are borne alternately. **FLOWERS** Borne in umbels in the axils of the leaves near the tips of the branches. They are attractive, very delicate and consist of four pure white petals (folded backwards around the pedicel) and a central mass of stamens, some of which are sterile and golden yellow, while the rest are fertile with golden-yellow bases and maroon tips (June–November). **FRUITS** Extremely spiny, brown, dehiscent capsules.

Flowers

Fruit

Crossberry (FSA463)

Grewia occidentalis var. *occidentalis*

Kruisbessie

Distribution & habitat It occurs from the winter-rainfall area of the Western Cape, north and northeastwards through the evergreen forests and coastal shrub of the southeastern Cape and the karroid scrub of the Karoo, to the scattered wooded areas in the Free State, through KwaZulu-Natal and northern South Africa to Mozambique and the eastern part of Zimbabwe. Crossberry is adapted to a divergent range of temperatures and rainfall.

Description It is mostly encountered as a multi-stemmed scrambler in sometimes dense thickets where it may reach a height of 6 m. In open woodland, it is a slender tree or shrub with a fairly dense crown and trailing branchlets. Its bark is grey-brown and fairly smooth. **LEAVES** Relatively large, rough to the touch (due to coarse hairs) and thin with conspicuously fine-toothed margins. **FLOWERS** The most outstanding feature of this plant. Most *Grewia* species have yellow flowers, a limited number have white and the minority (including this one) have showy, pale pink to mauve, star-shaped flowers that are about 35 mm in diameter. Flowering extends throughout most of spring and summer. **FRUITS** In accordance with the collective noun used for this group of plants (crossberries), fruits consist of four fruit lobes joined in the centre to form a rough square, or 'cross'. They are reddish brown when ripe.

(ZIMBABWE: (Z598) PINK DONKEYBERRY)

Notes: The trunks are too small to be of any use, apart from as firewood.

Fruit

Flower

Azanza (FSA466)

Azanza garckeana

Slymappel

Distribution & habitat In South Africa, this tree grows only in Limpopo. Further north, it occurs from eastern and northern Botswana and the Caprivi Strip, through Zimbabwe and Mozambique, to the east coast.

Description It is usually single-stemmed with a bushy crown and its branches often hang to the ground. It seldom reaches 10 m in height. The bark is greyish brown and fairly smooth, with small longitudinal ridges. The tree owes two of its other common names, slime- or snot-apple, to the glutinous slime produced when the fruit is chewed. **LEAVES** Simple, large (up to 200 × 200 mm) and three- to five-lobed with three or more major veins from the base. The upper surface is covered with coarse hairs while the underside has soft hairs. The petiole is long (up to 150 mm). **FLOWERS** Showy and yellow, they turn red when withering. Each crinkly petal has a maroon patch on the inside at the base. Petals are borne solitarily in leaf-axils near branch-ends. They flower over such a prolonged period (December–May) that the oldest fruit is nearly fully developed by the time the youngest flowers open. **FRUITS** Characteristic, nearly round capsules, up to 50 mm in diameter. They are longitudinally divided into five sections and covered with soft hairs. Fruits are olive-green, but turn yellow to brownish green at maturity (February–September).

(ZIMBABWE: (Z612) AZANZA)

Fruit

Flower

Trunk (compare size of human)

BRAAM VAN WYK

Baobab (FSA467)

Adansonia digitata

Kremetart

Distribution & habitat Because the baobab is not frost-resistant, it occurs only in the warmer, subtropical and tropical areas, including the northern area of Limpopo, further north and east, and in West Africa.

Description In height (up to 20 m), this species does not even come close to red mahogany (*Khaya anthotheca*), which is said to grow to 60 m, or to the yellowwoods (*Podocarpus*), which can reach approximately 40 m, but the size of the baobab's trunk is so great that it qualifies for first or second place, globally. Two particularly large trees occur near Gootsapan in Botswana and Chiramba in Mozambique. The South African record baobab grows near Sagole in Limpopo: height, 22 m; trunk diameter, 10.47 m. The smooth bark, sometimes heavily folded, is grey-brown to reddish brown. Under favourable conditions, some baobabs may live in excess of 1 000 years. Initially the growth rate is extremely fast, especially between 20 and 70 years, but during the latter period of its life, it slows down considerably. The trunk may even shrink during periods of severe drought. It is the only species representing the *Adansonia* genus native to Africa. **LEAVES** Palmately compound with five (seldom seven) leaflets, singular in the case of seedlings. **FLOWERS** Large and beautiful with their waxy, wrinkled petals; pollinated by bats. **FRUITS** Known in the herb and spice markets in Cairo as early as 2500 BC, when they were known as *bu hobab* (probably derived from the Arabic words *bu hibab* meaning 'fruit with many seeds').

(ZIMBABWE: (Z613) BAOBAB)

Left and above: flowers

Wildpear (FSA471)

Blompeer

Dombeya rotundifolia var. *rotundifolia*

Distribution & habitat Wildpear is the most abundant and the most widespread of the *Dombeya* species. It occurs from southern KwaZulu-Natal northwards and covers, with few exceptions, the entire Mozambique, Zimbabwe and northern parts of South Africa. It also features in the northern Free State, eastern and northern Botswana and the north-central area of Namibia. It is often associated with rocky situations. **Description** This deciduous tree cannot be overlooked in late winter/ early spring, when it is one of the first to start flowering. It is usually covered in white, and occasionally delicate pink, flowers. It is typically a single-stemmed, small (6 m), slender tree with a moderately spreading, sparse crown. Old stems are dark grey and often bear a few lateral twigs. The bark breaks up into small, irregular blocks. **LEAVES** Nearly circular, fairly large (up to 150 mm in diameter), seven-veined (from the base) and rough. The margin may be entirely to markedly, but irregularly, toothed. **FLOWERS** All the wildpear trees have attractive, showy and white to pink flowers. *D. pulchra* has the most beautiful flowers of all the species; its delicate petals are soft pink and each is adorned with a red patch on the inside of its base. **FRUITS** Small, yellowish brown, hairy nutlets, situated in the centre of the base of the cup formed by the dead, light brown and persistent petals.
(ZIMBABWE: (Z616) WILDPEAR)

Left: flowers
Above: aggregate fruit

African star-chestnut (FSA474)   *Sterculia africana* var. *africana*

Afrikasterkastaiing

Distribution & habitat This tree occurs from the Indian Ocean all along the Zambezi to the Caprivi Strip and Chobe area of Botswana. Isolated populations also exist in eastern Botswana, southwestern Zimbabwe and the north-central area of Namibia, with a tiny population fairly close to the Atlantic Ocean, next to the Kunene River.

Description This is not the largest among the star-chestnut trees, though it usually reaches a height of about 15 m. The colour varies from nearly white to reddish brown. Trunks are massive and smooth; outer bark flakes to reveal beautiful, pastel marbled underbark. **LEAVES** Large, three- to five-lobed, up to 150 × 130 mm, with five to seven large veins from the base; they are conspicuously hairy. **FLOWERS** Cup-shaped, greenish yellow with red lines, up to 25 mm in diameter and borne in compact, terminal racemes. The sexes are borne apart on the same tree, appearing in spring, before the leaves. **FRUITS** Impressive, they consist of 1–5 swollen carpels, up to 150 mm long, each with a prominent tip. They split on one side to release the seeds (March–April).

(ZIMBABWE: (Z618) TICKTREE; · NAMIBIA: STERCULIA)

90

Left: bark
Top: flowers & aggregate fruit
Above: aggregate fruit

Star-chestnut (FSA477)   *Sterculia rogersii*

Sterkastaiing

Distribution & habitat Star-chestnut is endemic to southern Africa. It is fairly abundant over its entire range, which roughly encompasses the area from the east of Botswana to the Mozambique coast, from Harare in the north, through Limpopo and Mpumalanga and into northern KwaZulu-Natal. It prefers well-drained situations and is found mostly on rocky outcrops.

Description It is a small (usually about 6 m), deciduous tree with an exceptionally thickset, succulent-like trunk, which always sub-divides low down. The crown is very sparse and spreads only moderately. It can sometimes be mistaken for a young baobab. The trunks are smooth, reddish brown and mottled with yellow or yellowish green patches caused by the peeling bark. Flowers and/or fruit can be found nearly all year round. **LEAVES** Simple, small, usually three-lobed and cordate (heart-shaped) to broadly ovate with a distinct cordate base. They are borne on new shoots only. **FLOWERS** Small, cup-shaped and borne on short, lateral shoots on branches. They are reddish green on the outside and yellowish green with red, vertical lines on the inside. **FRUITS** Swollen carpels, up to 80 mm in length and covered with golden hairs. Usually 3–5 will develop to maturity. Seeds are oval, smooth and dull leaden-grey.
(ZIMBABWE: (Z621) STAR-CHESTNUT)

91

Top left: flowers
Top right: fruit
Above: bark

Peeling plane (FSA483)

Lekkerbreek

Ochna pulchra subsp. *pulchra*

Distribution & habitat This species occurs from the Magaliesberg range north and northeastwards into Zimbabwe, as well as west into the southeast of Botswana. It is also abundant in northern Botswana and northeastern Namibia.

Description It is a single-stemmed, deciduous tree with a moderately dense, roundish crown. Usually between 6 and 7 m high, it mostly occurs as a shrub in dense thickets. Twigs and branches are extremely brittle and nearly white. Old stems are smooth, cream-coloured and usually almost completely covered by thin, hard, curled flakes of peeling bark. Very old stems are dark grey and the bark peels in small, flat sections. **LEAVES** Simple and borne at twig terminals. New leaves are very glossy and can be pale green, brownish green or even red-brown. Mature leaves may be up to 100 mm in length; they are glossy, hard and brittle. Leaf margins are usually entire but sometimes finely serrate in the upper third. **FLOWERS** Up to 20 mm in diameter, pale yellow and borne in masses (August–October). **FRUITS** Borne in pendent clusters and change colour from pale or olive-green to pitch-black.

(ZIMBABWE: (Z636) PEELING-BARK PLANE)

Flowers

Fruit

African mangosteen (FSA486)

Garcinia livingstonei

Afrikageelmelkhout

Distribution & habitat This species occurs from northern KwaZulu-Natal northwards through Mozambique, Swaziland and the lowveld of Mpumalanga and Limpopo to southeastern Zimbabwe. It reappears along the Zambezi River from Mozambique to the Caprivi Strip and in northwestern Zimbabwe and northern Botswana.

Description It is a handsome, distinctive, evergreen tree (up to 12 m). Although single-stemmed, it often splits into two or more secondary stems low down. Branches are rigid; in full-grown trees, the crown is invariably topped by long shoots sticking out above the canopy. Old bark is grey to black and subdivided into small, regular sections. This species contains yellow latex, which is also exuded by the veins when leaves are cracked across. **LEAVES** Occur in verticils of three and persist even on fairly thick branches. They are simple, red and soft when young, but hard, dark green, thick and brittle when mature. The veins are clearly visible since they are yellow-green. **FLOWERS** Small, pale green to yellowish green and borne in small groups in leaf-axils on older branchlets (September–November). Male and bisexual flowers are borne on separate trees. **FRUITS** As can be seen in the illustration, they are very striking, up to about 35 mm in diameter and produced in profusion.

(**ZIMBABWE:** (Z646) AFRICAN MANGOSTEEN)

Notes: The fruit is edible and is enjoyed by people and animals alike; an alcoholic beverage is also prepared from it.

Top: fruit
Above: bark

Yellow helicopter (FSA486.5)

Monotes glaber

Geelpapierkelk

Distribution & habitat The *Monotes* genus is the only one in the Dipterocarpaceae (meaning 'winged fruit') family represented in the tree flora of southern Africa. Apart from Zimbabwe, *M. glaber* can be seen only in the east and northeast of Botswana, and has been found a few kilometres south of Kazangula in Botswana, which is farther north than its previously known range in that country; more fieldwork may reveal its existence in the Caprivi Strip as well. It grows in fairly dense to open woodland on sandy soil.

Description This is a small to medium-sized tree with a dense, wide-spreading crown. It is probably deciduous. The bark is grey-brown and fairly smooth. LEAVES Simple, oblong to elliptic, up to 100 mm long (usually 70 mm), glossy and light green; the yellowish veins are conspicuous. A characteristic and distinctive spot (nectary) occurs at the base of the midrib. FLOWERS Star-like, pale greenish yellow and borne in lax, relatively few-flowered axillary heads (20–40 mm long), which appear between November and March. FRUITS Slightly oval, ridged, about 10 mm in diameter and situated in the centre of the five persistent calyx lobes, which are wing-like and straw-coloured when ripe, giving the impression of a wooden star-like flower. They are up to 30 mm long.

(ZIMBABWE: (Z648) YELLOW HELICOPTER)

Notes: The timber is light brown with darker striations; it is suitable for the manufacture of furniture.

Flower

Fruit

Snuffbox-tree (FSA492)   *Oncoba spinosa*

Snuifkalbassie

Distribution & habitat This is a tropical species occurring as far south as KwaZulu-Natal, though it is not abundant anywhere in South Africa. In Zimbabwe, it tends to form thickets. Available information points to its presence in Swaziland, Mozambique, Mpumalanga and Limpopo, as well as all along the Zambezi into a limited area of northeastern Botswana and the Caprivi district of Namibia. Judging from its habitat preference in the Mpumalanga lowveld, it prefers moist conditions, such as riverbanks.

Description The snuffbox-tree is semi-deciduous to deciduous, usually multi-stemmed, with a dense crown; it is up to 6 m in height and armed with fairly long, thin, solitary spines. The bark is greyish brown and rather smooth. It usually only attains shrub size and is therefore an unknown entity among local dendrologists. **LEAVES** Big (up to 120 × 60 mm – though usually somewhat smaller), simple, thin leathery and ovate. **FLOWERS** The most outstanding assets are the beautiful, sweetly scented flowers. They may be up to 100 mm in diameter with a large number of pure white, crinkled petals and a central mass of yellow stamens (the whole resembles a fried egg). They are borne solitarily and axillary or terminally (September–January). **FRUITS** Spherical, hard-shelled, up to 60 mm in diameter, indehiscent and brown when mature. The brown seeds are embedded in a dry, yellow, edible pulp. (ZIMBABWE: (Z656) FRIED-EGG FLOWER)

Notes: The wood is light brown and hard but is seldom used, as large pieces are not available. When the fruit is dry, the seeds rattle inside it. These dried fruits are used to amuse small children and are attached to anklets and bracelets for dancers. They are also used as snuffboxes.

BRAAM VAN WYK

Left: male flowers
Top: fruit
Above: fruit & seeds

Wildpeach (FSA494)

Kiggelaria africana

Wildeperske

Distribution & habitat This is one of the larger trees, attaining a height of up to 25 m when it grows in the evergreen forests from the southern Cape to the Soutpansberg, the Mutare region of Zimbabwe and the adjoining Mozambican territory. However, in the more arid regions of Namaqualand, the Western Cape, the Karoo, the Free State, Lesotho, the interior of KwaZulu-Natal, the northern provinces of South Africa and southeastern Botswana, it is much smaller.

Description It is a single-stemmed tree with a wide-spreading crown, when found in suitable habitats. The trunk is straight and sometimes very long. The bark is smooth and pale brown when young, becoming dark brown and flaky when old. **LEAVES** Simple, oblong to elliptic, up to 90 × 50 mm (though more often smaller) and softly hairy when young, but later glabrous. The margins may be entire or markedly serrate, sometimes in the upper half only. Small warts occur in the axils of the secondary veins. **FLOWERS** Male flowers, borne in sparse heads, and female flowers, borne solitarily, occur on separate trees. They are 10 mm in diameter and yellowish green to greenish white (August–January). **FRUITS** Characteristic, spherical capsules, up to 20 mm in diameter. They are rough and greyish green, splitting into four valves at maturity. The black seeds are covered with an orange-red, sticky coating. These fruits are eaten by birds.

(ZIMBABWE: (Z673) WILDPEACH)

Far left: flowers
Left: fruit
Above: fruit

Mountain hardpear (FSA514) — *Olinia emarginata*

Berghardepeer

Distribution & habitat In southern Africa, this genus is represented by seven tree species. They share one extraordinary characteristic: all have a rather limited distribution. Six are South African (although *O. rochetiana* is a tropical species) and occur largely on the eastern side of the country. The seventh is limited to eastern Zimbabwe and possibly Mozambique. *O. emarginata* has the widest distribution. It extends from the Eastern Cape, through Lesotho, KwaZulu-Natal, the eastern Free State and Swaziland to the bushveld areas north of the Magaliesberg, but not reaching the Soutpansberg or the lowveld. It is therefore very well adapted to a wide range of varying ecological conditions, from coastal to montane.

Description In a suitable habitat like the evergreen forests, it is a large tree (up to 20 m) with a single stem and a dense, wide-spreading crown. The bark is light grey on young branches, becoming dark grey and finely, longitudinally ridged when older.

LEAVES Simple and borne in opposite pairs, the leaves are smallish (up to 50 mm long), elliptic, glossy and exceptionally dark green on the upper surface, while pale green below.

FLOWERS Small, pink and borne in axillary heads during the summer. **FRUITS** Occur in small, dense clusters. Glossy, nearly spherical and attractively dark red when ripe (March–June), they are the most conspicuous part of this tree.

Flowers

Flowers

Pompontree (FSA521)

Dais cotinifolia

Kannabas

Distribution & habitat This attractive, deciduous tree is largely confined to South Africa; it occurs from the Eastern Cape, north along the coast and far inland, through Lesotho, KwaZulu-Natal and Swaziland, as well as into the northern provinces, where it mainly occurs along the Drakensberg range up to the Soutpansberg. In Zimbabwe, it is restricted to a small area in the south, as well as the Chimanimani area in the east, where it crosses over into Mozambique. It mainly grows at the margins of forests or in bush on rocky hillsides.

Description It is usually a very slender tree of about 5 m in height (though a height of 10–12 m is possible), but in favourable, open conditions, the crown may spread rather wide. Its bark is smooth and brownish grey. The flowering period may be any time between early summer and autumn, depending on the climate of the area. **LEAVES** Simple, medium-sized (up to 100 × 60 mm) and arranged in precise opposite pairs. New leaves are light green; older leaves are bluish green, turning yellow to brown before being shed. **FLOWERS** The tree's greatest assets, they are tubular, up to 30 mm long, pink to pinkish mauve and are borne in dense, nearly spherical terminal heads, which are up to 40 mm in diameter. They remain showy for about three weeks; when they die, they turn grey and later black, but remain on the tree for a long time. **FRUITS** Minute nutlets. The shield-like bracts at the base of the inflorescences become hard upon death, yet persist on the tree for over a year.

(ZIMBABWE: (Z683) POMPONTREE)

Notes: High-quality rope is produced from the bark.

Top: flowers
Above: fruit

Red bushwillow (FSA532)

Combretum apiculatum subsp. *apiculatum*

Rooiboswilg

Distribution & habitat This is a particularly common tree in the northern part of the subcontinent, occurring in all countries and as far south as northern KwaZulu-Natal in the east and central Namibia in the west. It avoids very arid areas, as well as those where winter temperatures may be low. This species only grows in fairly well-drained, sandy, gravelly or rocky situations. In a favourable habitat it is often the dominant or co-dominant woody species.

Description Red bushwillow is a small, deciduous tree with a short stem; it usually subdivides low down, or it may have more than one stem from ground level. The crown has a fairly wide spread, but is sparse. It seldom surpasses 8 or 9 m in height, though one of 14 m was measured at Kubu Lodge in Botswana. Old stems are grey to greyish black and the bark cracks shallowly into small, irregular sections, which may peel off in thin flakes. **LEAVES** Simple and usually borne in decussate pairs, they are elliptic, often obovate, and characterized by curved or twisted, tapering tips; young leaves are glossy. **FLOWERS** Small, pale, fragrant, yellowish green florets borne in axillary spikes (August–November). Flower buds are often reddish purple. **FRUITS** Typically four-winged, roughly oval and, on average, 25 × 20 mm. The colour of the fruit changes from green, through red-brown to dark brown. Seeds contain a chemical substance that causes severe hiccupping when eaten.
(ZIMBABWE: (Z692) GLOSSY BUSHWILLOW; NAMIBIA: KUDUBUSH)

Notes: The well-known timber is claimed by many to be the best for barbecue purposes. It is extremely heavy, hard and strong. The leaves of this tree are browsed by game.

Centre: flowers
Left: fruit
Above: bark

Leadwood (FSA539)   *Combretum imberbe*

Hardekool

Distribution & habitat This is the largest of some 40 tree species/subspecies of the *Combretum* genus found in southern Africa. Leadwood has, with minor exceptions, the same distribution as the red bushwillow, but is nowhere as abundant and prefers soils with high clay content.

Description It is a deciduous tree, most often having a single trunk and a wide-spreading, sparse crown. The timber is exceptionally heavy (approximately 1 200 kg per cubic metre) and very hard – hence the common name. Old bark is pale grey to greyish black and cracks into small, flat, irregular blocks. Some years back, the trunk of a dead tree in Swaziland was carbon dated by the Council for Scientific and Industrial Research (CSIR) in Pretoria: although it was far less than a metre in diameter at ground level, its age was determined to be about 1 000 years. It was estimated to have been dead for about 150 years, yet it was still standing upright. **LEAVES** Simple, mostly smallish (35 × 17 mm), elliptic to narrowly obovate, glabrous, conspicuously undulating and grey-green, due to a dense cover of silvery, microscopic scales. They are usually arranged in decussate pairs. **FLOWERS** Small, greenish white to yellowish green and borne in sparse, axillary panicles (November–December). **FRUITS** Four-winged and occur singly or in small groups. They are nearly spherical, small (to 15 mm in diameter), initially pale green and buff-coloured when mature. (ZIMBABWE: (Z706) LEADWOOD)

Notes: The wood is fine-grained and dark brown to black in colour; it is virtually impossible to work with.

BRAAM VAN WYK

Left: flowers
Above: fruit

Flamecreeper (FSA545)

Combretum microphyllum

Vlamklimop

Distribution & habitat It occurs at the margins of evergreen forests, in high-rainfall areas and at low altitudes, such as the lowveld areas of Zimbabwe, Limpopo, Mpumalanga and Swaziland. It is always in riverbeds, where it scrambles over neighbouring trees and shrubs to form thickets. Apart from the areas mentioned, the flamecreeper mainly grows in northern KwaZulu-Natal, large parts of Mozambique and most of Zimbabwe.
Description This is not a tree in the true sense of the word: it is a vigorous and robust climber. With the assistance of its neighbours, it can reach a height of 15 m, possibly more. It is very conspicuous and spectacular when in flower. Old bark is pale greyish brown and flakes in old specimens only. Emergence of the flowers (long before the leaves) is a sure sign of spring approaching. According to locals, it heralds the new season for tigerfish-anglers. **LEAVES** Simple, fairly large, glossy, dark green and borne in opposite pairs; they are dropped in winter. The basal section of the petiole remains intact and develops into a blunt spine. **FLOWERS** Individual, crimson-red and small, they are produced in such quantities that the trailing branches look like large sprays (August–September). Stamens are the most conspicuous components of the flowers, as the petals are very small. **FRUITS** Typically four-winged (rarely five-winged), smallish (20 mm diameter) and change colour – from very light green through pink and dark red-brown to pale yellow.
(ZIMBABWE: (Z708) BURNINGBUSH)

Far left: fruit
Left: flowers

Stink-bushwillow (FSA547)   *Pteleopsis myrtifolia*

Stinkboswilg

Distribution & habitat In South Africa, this tree occurs only in Maputaland in northern KwaZulu-Natal and in the extreme northeastern corner of Limpopo. In Zimbabwe, it is restricted to a fairly narrow region along the border, except in the southwest. It features only in the far northeast of Botswana and the eastern extremity of the Caprivi Strip, but is widespread in Mozambique. It is found mainly in dense woodland on deep sand.

Description It is most often encountered as a multi-stemmed shrub, but may grow into a fairly large tree (15 m) with a bare trunk and a wide-spreading crown, which is characterized by slender, pendent branchlets. The colour of the bark on branches and stems varies from almost white (sunny side) to dark grey, or even black. Old bark forms longitudinal ridges. It is deciduous.

LEAVES Simple and borne alternately, sub-opposite or opposite; they are rather small (usually up to 30 mm long), dark green, glabrous above and pale green with pubescence below.

FLOWERS Small, white and strongly, unpleasantly scented; they are borne in short axillary heads (October–February, depending on rainfall).

FRUITS Borne in pendent clusters. They are small (up to 20 mm long), oval to orbicular and mostly two-winged, but may have three (sometimes four) thin, pergamentaceous wings.
(ZIMBABWE: (Z720) TWO-WINGED STINK-BUSHWILLOW; NAMIBIA: TWO-WINGED STINKBUSH)

Flowers

Fruit

Small clusterleaf (FSA550.1)

Terminalia randii

Kleintrosblaar

Distribution & habitat The small clusterleaf occurs in the eastern and northern areas of Botswana, the eastern tip of the Caprivi Strip and the west of Zimbabwe. It does not occur in South Africa. In Botswana's Kasane area, it grows on the dry, rocky hillsides; elsewhere, apparently, it also grows on barren, stony ground and black soils.

Description The tree is medium-sized, barely reaching 10 m in height. It is single-stemmed, often branching fairly low. The crown has a poor spread and even small twigs are very rigid; branches freely – each branch, with its twigs, tends to form a layer. Bark is grey and longitudinally fissured. In southern Africa, this is the only species of *Terminalia* with thorns. **LEAVES** Small, narrowly obovate and occur in clusters in the axils of the short, sharp thorns. **FLOWERS** Small, white, sweetly scented and borne in short (30 mm), sparse spikes together with leaves (November–April). **FRUITS** Probably the smallest of all *Terminalia* species: up to 25 × 12 mm, though usually smaller. They consist of a typical, hard, woody fruit covered by a thin, pergamentaceous wing. When young, they are purplish, but turn pale brown when dry. They are borne on slender stalks, which break easily, though some may remain on the tree until the following flowering season. **(ZIMBABWE: (Z725)** SMALL CLUSTERLEAF)

Fruit

Flowers

Silver clusterleaf (FSA551)

Terminalia sericea

Vaalboom

Distribution & habitat Silver clusterleaf is one of the most abundant trees in southern Africa. It occurs over very large tracts of land in all four northern countries of the subcontinent, in addition to the northern provinces of South Africa, Swaziland and northern KwaZulu-Natal. Wherever the habitat is suitable it thrives and is invariably the dominant tree, forming dense, often homogeneous stands. It has a strong preference for well-drained, sandy soil. **Description** This species is usually not more than about 8 m high. Stems are comparatively short, pale to dark grey with the bark splitting lengthwise to form ridges. Young trees are slender. With age, the crown spreads and often tends to be flat. This tree is deciduous. **LEAVES** Simple and borne on new growth only, occurring close together at the tips of twigs. They are narrowly obovate, up to 100 × 25 mm and are – particularly when young – covered by silky hairs, which give them a silvery sheen. **FLOWERS** Small (4 mm), off-white to yellowish and borne in fairly long spikes among the leaves. They have a nauseating smell. **FRUITS** Flat, roughly oval in shape, measuring up to 35 mm in length and borne in clusters. It consists of a hard, thickened inner portion with a stiff, thin, undulating wing around it. Young fruit is pubescent, but the hairs are gradually lost. The colour changes from buff-green, through a striking pale red (sunny side) to pale brown at maturity. (ZIMBABWE: (Z727) SILVER CLUSTERLEAF)

Left: flowers
Above: fruit

Woodland waterberry (FSA557)   *Syzygium guineense* subsp. *guineense*

Bosveldwaterbessie

Distribution & habitat This species varies greatly in different areas. It occurs on the eastern side of South Africa from KwaZulu-Natal northwards, including Swaziland and the western side of Mozambique, into Zimbabwe, then westwards to Botswana and the Caprivi Strip; there is a small population in northern Namibia. The woodland waterberry is an evergreen tree and nearly always grows in moist conditions, sometimes even in water.

Description It is single-stemmed and usually not more than 9 or 10 m high, but it can grow to double that size in forests. **LEAVES** Simple, fairly big (up to 140 mm long) and borne in decussate pairs; their upper surface is glossy and pale green to darkish green (but never as green as those of *S. cordatum* with which it is often associated). The veins are mostly yellowish green, but sometimes red. The prominent yellowish petioles may be up to 30 mm long. **FLOWERS** White, sweetly scented and borne in terminal clusters, they resemble those of the guava and some Australian blue gums. The white stamens are their most attractive and visible component. **FRUITS** Oval berries, usually up to 20 mm long (those in the picture are 45 mm) and dark purple or maroon when ripe; on trees at Chobe, they are often bicoloured. Berries are fleshy and edible: wild animals relish them.

(ZIMBABWE: (Z736) WOODLAND WATERBERRY; NAMIBIA: WATERPEAR)

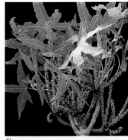
Flowers

Fruit

Rock cabbagetree (FSA562)

Cussonia natalensis

Rotskiepersol

Distribution & habitat The rock cabbagetree has a fairly wide distribution: its range encompasses KwaZulu-Natal, Swaziland, Mpumalanga, Limpopo, the eastern corner of Botswana and a relatively wide strip across Zimbabwe to the northeastern border with Mozambique. It prefers a rocky habitat.

Description It is a small (7 m), deciduous tree with a short, thickset trunk and a wide-spreading, rounded crown. Up to now, the largest specimen measured in South Africa is 10.5 m high (in Mokopane). The ends of the branches are similar to those of other *Cussonia* species: they are exceptionally thick, soft and succulent-like. Old trunks are grey and their corky bark is deeply grooved longitudinally. The ridges are broken up into rectangular sections by crosswise cracks. **LEAVES** Simple, borne spirally (usually close together at tips of branches) and deeply five-lobed. Occasionally, some lobes do not develop fully. The whole leaf is about 150 mm in diameter. Margins are conspicuously serrate. **FLOWERS** Inflorescences borne terminally on leafless lateral shoots. When young, they resemble mediaeval maces. They consist of a large number of short spikes on which the sessile florets are closely packed. They have an unpleasant smell. **FRUITS** Small, round, fleshy and purplish red when ripe. (ZIMBABWE: (Z749) SIMPLE-LEAVED CABBAGETREE)

Notes: The timber is soft and pale brown; it is not used.

Top: fruit
Middle: flowers
Above: bark

Carrot-tree (FSA569)

Steganotaenia araliacea var. *araliacea*

Geelwortelboom

Distribution & habitat The carrot-tree is fairly rare and never abundant, but occurs over a wide range of territory, stretching from Swaziland through Mpumalanga and Limpopo, into eastern Botswana, as well as western and southern Zimbabwe. It also grows in an area in the vicinity of Harare and northern Botswana, and in the northern half of Namibia. Palgrave (2005) states that it is 'more characteristic of low altitude woodland, also on rocky outcrops', but in South Africa it grows only in rocky areas, such as outcrops and hillsides.

Description It is a deciduous tree with a single, short, bare trunk and an extremely sparse crown; it may reach 8 m in height, but is usually smaller. Young twigs are thick, very brittle and succulent-like. The stem and branches are smooth, bright yellow-green or yellowish grey and the bark peels off in thin, chartaceous flakes. On very old stems, bark is corky and horizontally cracked. All parts of the tree have the familiar 'carrot' smell. **LEAVES** Imparipinnately compound and borne close together at the branch ends. They are characterized by dentate margins, with the 'teeth' ending in thin, soft mucros. Leaflets are a bright pale green; they are very thin and soft. **FLOWERS** Tiny, yellowish and borne in compound umbels (July–November); they strongly resemble those of the carrot, which is how this species came by its common name. **FRUITS** Small, flat, two-winged capsules. (ZIMBABWE: (Z754) POPGUN-TREE)

Fruit

Flowers

Cape-beech (FSA578)

Rapanea melanophloeos

Kaapse boekenhout

Distribution & habitat The Cape-beech is a constituent of the evergreen forests on the eastern side of the subcontinent in the area between the coast and the escarpment, ranging from Cape Town to northeastern Limpopo (Drakensberg) and in the east and north of Zimbabwe, extending into a small portion of Mozambique. Since it is a tropical species, it also features in countries north of the Zambezi. It is abundant in evergreen forests, as well as the drier coastal forests.

Description This tree may reach a height of 25 m but is normally much smaller. It is mostly single-stemmed; young stems are whitish pink with small, corky knobs while older trunks may have large, roundish knobs. With age, the bark becomes corky, longitudinally fissured and greyish brown. In forests, the crowns of young trees are long and slender, only spreading when reaching the forest canopy. The wood has a reticulated grain, very similar to that of members of the protea family (Proteaceae). Flowers and fruits are often found at the same time of year. **LEAVES** Simple, fairly large (up to 140 × 40 mm) and clustered at the twig terminals, they are dark green above and paler below; margins are rolled under. Petioles are distinctive: they are grooved above and always coloured red to purple. **FLOWERS** Male and female flowers are borne on different trees (winter to middle summer). They are small, greenish cream and occur in masses in the leaf-axils; they are mostly on older wood below the leaves. **FRUITS** Small, spherical fruits that often occur in such large quantities that the twigs are completely covered. They are crowded close to branchlets and change colour from green to white and purple when ripe.

(ZIMBABWE: (Z766) CAPE-BEECH)

Far left and left: fruit
Above: flowers

White-milkwood (FSA579)

Sideroxylon inerme subsp. *inerme*

Witmelkhout

Distribution & habitat White-milkwood is primarily a coastal species throughout the greatest part of its range, which extends from the Cape Peninsula to the north of KwaZulu-Natal; from there it spreads out to include the interior of southern Mozambique, the lowveld of Mpumalanga and Limpopo and southern Zimbabwe.

Description It is a smallish evergreen tree or shrub; as a tree, this species may grow up to 10 m in height. It is very dense, dark green and has a single stem, which branches low (branches usually rest on the ground) and a very wide-spreading crown. It contains milky latex. This is a protected species in South Africa and three specimens have been declared national monuments. The best known of these is the Post Office Tree in Mossel Bay, which could be more than 600 years old. The other is in Woodstock in the Western Cape and is called the Treaty Tree. The third is near Peddie in the Eastern Cape. **LEAVES** Simple, roughly elliptic, on average 80 × 30 mm, thick, hard, glossy and dark green. **FLOWERS** Inconspicuous, greenish white, small and borne either solitarily or in clusters. They are found in leaf-axils or on leafless older branches (from September to April). **FRUITS** Spherical, smooth, glossy berries, roughly 10 mm in diameter; they turn black upon ripening. The layer of fruit pulp is relatively thick and contains latex. (ZIMBABWE: (Z768; SUBSP. *DIOSPYROIDES*) NORTHERN WHITE-MILKWOOD)

Notes: The timber is heavy, very hard, pale brown, finely textured and durable; it has been put to many uses.

Far right: flowers
Right: fruit

Stemfruit (FSA581)

Englerophytum magalismontanum

Stamvrug

Distribution & habitat This species, previously named *Bequaertiodendron magalismontanum*, occurs in all the mountainous regions of northern KwaZulu-Natal and Swaziland, throughout the northern provinces of South Africa and in the southeast of Botswana. It is locally common in evergreen forests, woods or ravines and along riverbanks, especially among rocks in sandy soil in eastern Zimbabwe and on the Mozambique side of the border.

Description On mountains, it is a smallish tree (5 m) but in forests, it can grow to at least 10 m. The trunk is short and frequently crooked; the very dark green crown is spreading and generally dense. Young twigs are conspicuously rusty-brown due to a dense layer of hairs. The bark on the trunks and branches is fairly smooth, but is covered with small, brown to blackish protuberances, on which the flowers and fruit are borne. **LEAVES** Simple and borne relatively far apart, especially in young plants, they persist even on thick branchlets. They are fairly big (up to 150 × 56 mm), very dark green, glossy above and buff-brown and tomentose underneath. **FLOWERS** Fragrant, small and cream-coloured, they appear in small clusters on the trunk and branches, as well as in leaf-axils. **FRUITS** Elliptic, up to 25 mm in length and orange to deep maroon when ripe (December). (ZIMBABWE: (Z773) STEMFRUIT)

Notes: Wild animals, especially primates, relish the fruit. It is rich in vitamin C and is used to produce vinegar, wine and syrup.

Left: fruit
Above: flowers

Coastal red-milkwood (FSA583)

Mimusops caffra

Kusrooimelkhout

Distribution & habitat It is one of the important, sometimes dominant, constituents of the coastal dune vegetation, roughly found from East London to as far north as Beira in Mozambique. As the common name implies, this tree occurs only along the coast. This is a very hardy plant, which can tolerate strong winds and salt spray from the sea so well that it even occurs in thickets down to the high-tide mark, as is markedly illustrated, for instance, at Chintsa Mouth near East London.

Description Although it often occurs in large shrub form, it can be a large tree (15 m) with a single trunk and a very dense and wide-spreading crown. The bark, even on old stems, is fairly smooth and only longitudinally cracked. It is grey to dark grey with white patches. Young branchlets and leaves are covered with dark, rusty-brown hairs. It is evergreen. **LEAVES** Simple, obovate-oblong, up to 70 mm long, with a prominent petiole; they are hard, glossy and dark green above, while pale green with conspicuous hairs below. **FLOWERS** White, star-shaped and borne in small groups in the axils of terminal leaves. Sepals are covered with rusty-brown hairs. **FRUITS** Oval berries, up to 20 mm in length, which become attractively orange-red when ripe; they are edible and tasty.

Notes: The reddish timber is finely grained, heavy, hard and durable. It is used for boat-building. As with the other *Mimusops* species, it contains latex.

Left: flowers
Above: fruit

Ebony guarri (FSA598)

Euclea pseudebenus

Ebbehoutghwarrie

Distribution & habitat A variety of common names are used to describe this tree, but all of them contain the common denominator 'ebony', which refers to the black heartwood. This rather unusual, graceful tree is drought-resistant and frost-tolerant; it occurs in the very arid western areas of the subcontinent from the Northern Cape (mainly along the Orange River, west of Upington) up to the northern Namibian border.

Description Old stems are dark grey. The bark breaks up into fairly large, thin flakes, which sometimes peel off. This tree is mostly multi-stemmed from ground level. The crown is very dense and is characterized by long, slender, drooping branches. It is evergreen. **LEAVES** Narrow, slender (up to 50 × 5 mm), slightly curved and arranged spirally; they are leathery, yellowish green and may be softly hairy when young. **FLOWERS** Very small, greenish and borne in small, axillary clusters; they usually appear in August–September, though sometimes much later. **FRUITS** Small (5 mm), spherical and produced in masses, they remain on the tree for an extended period. They change from pale green, through red to nearly black. Although edible, and eaten by wild animals, they are not very tasty.
(NAMIBIA: WILD-EBONY)

Notes: The wood is beautiful, hard, durable, fine-grained and black. It is suitable for various commodities, but trunks are often too small to be useful.

Top: flowers
Above left: spring leaves
Above right: fruit

Jackalberry (FSA606)

Diospyros mespiliformis

Jakkalsbessie

Distribution & habitat The jackalberry is a tropical species occurring in all countries of southern Africa, except Lesotho. In South Africa, it is limited to northern KwaZulu-Natal and the lowveld of Mpumalanga and Limpopo. It is also found in northeastern Namibia, which is an area with high rainfall. It prefers moist conditions and therefore grows most often along rivers and streams; it is often associated with termite mounds.

Description It is a fairly large, deciduous tree (up to 20 m) with a single, long, fluted trunk and a very dense, wide-spreading crown. Old stems are grey to black; bark breaks up and peels off in small, flat sections. **LEAVES** Simple, initially pale green or pale brown and later dark green; they are usually oblong and up to 80 × 30 mm. **FLOWERS** Cream-coloured to white, tubiform and bell-shaped. They are unisexual and borne in leaf-axils on separate trees; female flowers are borne singly (December). **FRUITS** Spherical berries, about 20 mm in diameter and yellow when ripe. A persistent calyx partially covers each berry at its base. The fruit pulp is jelly-like, edible and tasty. Berries remain on the tree for a long time and are often seen on leafless trees during spring.

(ZIMBABWE: (Z796) AFRICAN EBONY, JACKALBERRY)

Notes: Dry timber is pale red with a brownish tinge. Fairly hard and durable, it was extensively used in the wagon-building trade.

BRAAM VAN WYK

Left: flowers
Top and above: fruit

Bladdernut (FSA611)

Diospyros whyteana

Swartbas

Distribution & habitat Although this is a tropical species, occurring north of the Zambezi and widespread throughout South Africa, it is only found in a relatively small area in Zimbabwe. It has not been recorded in Namibia, Botswana or Mozambique. In South Africa, its range extends from the Cape Peninsula along the east coast, as well as quite far inland, through KwaZulu-Natal, Lesotho and the eastern Free State to the northern provinces, where it is widespread.

Description Under favourable conditions, the bladdernut may be attractive enough to be a garden subject – particularly as it is evergreen. Although sometimes single-stemmed, it is usually multi-stemmed with a spreading, dense crown. It may grow to 7 m in height. **LEAVES** Quite distinctive: simple, usually ovate to oblong, up to 45 × 25 mm, borne alternately, very dark green and strikingly shiny above, while pale green and hairy below. Margins are fringed with hairs. **FLOWERS** White to cream, fragrant and borne in short axillary sprays (August–November); the sexes are separate. **FRUITS** Unique, borne singly, roughly round and up to 20 mm in diameter; they turn red when mature. They are completely enclosed by the sepals, which enlarge considerably and become fused to form a longitudinally segmented bladder; sepals remain on the tree long after the fruit has fallen.

(ZIMBABWE: (Z802) BLADDERNUT)

114

Flowers

Fruit

Wild jasmine (FSA612)   *Schrebera alata*

Wildejasmyn

Distribution & habitat This is a tropical species. It occurs as far south as KwaZulu-Natal, including Swaziland, Mozambique (south and north), Limpopo, Mpumalanga and the eastern part of Zimbabwe.

Description Wild jasmine usually reaches a height of about 8 m, but in evergreen forest it may be twice as high. The only officially measured specimen in South Africa is 20 m high, but its spread is only 6.9 m. It is a deciduous tree with a rather sparse, upright, rounded crown and a single, short, grooved stem. The bark is grey-brown and soft, but rough. It breaks up into small, irregular sections. The wood is pale to reddish brown, hard and durable. When the living wood is exposed through debarking, it turns bright purple and later dark brown. The timber is often damaged by woodborers and even thin twigs are often hollow. **LEAVES** Borne in decussate pairs; imparipinnately compound with two (seldom one) pairs of leaflets. The petiole and rachis are distinctive, as they usually have conspicuous lateral wings (fillodes). **FLOWERS** Beautiful, sweetly scented and borne in axillary and terminal cymes (September–February). They are trumpet-shaped, about 15 mm long and white, pale to intensely pink and dark red at the base of the petals. **FRUITS** Hard, woody, glabrous, wedge-shaped capsules, which split lengthwise while on the tree and persist for some time. The flat seeds are winged.

(ZIMBABWE: (Z804) WING-LEAVED WOODEN-PEAR)

115

Flowers

Fruit

Wild olive (FSA617)   *Olea europaea* subsp. *africana*

Olienhout

Distribution & habitat It is one of only a few tree species to be found almost throughout South Africa. It also occurs in southern Mozambique, the western part of Namibia and fairly large areas of Zimbabwe. It is rare in Botswana and is apparently limited to the southeastern sections.

Description The wild olive is drought-resistant and frost-tolerant. It is a single-stemmed, evergreen tree with a moderately spreading crown. Old trunks are nearly always fluted, dented or knobby. The largest tree thus far measured in South Africa (in the Brits district) is 17 m high. The crown-spread of most of the trees measured does not exceed 17 m; stem diameter varies between 0.9 and 1.5 m. **LEAVES** Simple, quite small, narrowly oblong or oval and borne in decussate pairs (even on thickish branchlets). The upper surface is glossy, buff-green to dark green with small, grey stipules; the underside is brownish green, dull and covered with silvery or brownish scales. The margin is always rolled under (revolute). **FLOWERS** Small, white and borne in loose, axillary or terminal clusters (November–December). **FRUITS** Small and slightly oval, they are initially green with white spots, but change to yellow and purplish black when ripe. Birds and other animals eat the fruit, despite its bitterness.

(ZIMBABWE: (Z810) AFRICAN OLIVE)

Notes: The finely textured timber is used to manufacture furniture. This tree is highly recommended as a garden plant.

Flowers

Fruit

Small ironwood (FSA618)

Olea capensis subsp. *capensis*

Kleinysterhout

Distribution & habitat Of the six different olive trees in southern Africa (three of which are subspecies of *O. capensis*), four are practically endemic to South Africa. This particular tree is one of those and is mostly found on the coastal side of the escarpment, roughly from Clanwilliam in the Western Cape to the Cape Peninsula and eastwards and northwards to southern KwaZulu-Natal. It is abundant in both wet and dry shrub forests, with the main focus of its distribution in the area between East London and Cape Town.

Description Small ironwood is one of the highly variable trees. It often occurs as a bushy shrub, barely reaching 10 m in the Knysna/ Tsitsikamma area; however, on the slopes of Table Mountain, it is a large tree. Its stem may be relatively thin, often crooked to long, thick and straight; it is fairly smooth for quite a long time. With age, the bark becomes rough and corky. It is an evergreen tree with a very dense crown. When growing in the open, branching may be low down, with the lowest branches on the ground. **LEAVES** Broadly elliptic (up to 100 mm long), hard, smooth and leathery, dark green, glossy above and pale green beneath. The leaf margins are entire and conspicuously rolled under. **FLOWERS** Very small, white, sweetly scented and borne in many-flowered, terminal or axillary heads (July–February, depending on climatic conditions). **FRUITS** Almost spherical to ovoid, up to 10 mm long, fleshy, become purple when ripe.

Notes: The wood is widely used in the furniture industry.

Flowers

Fruit

Black bitterberry (FSA630)

Strychnos potatorum

Swartbitterbessie

Distribution & habitat It covers the bigger portion of Zimbabwe and is common in some regions of Mozambique, the Kasane/Chobe area in Botswana and the Caprivi Strip. In South Africa, it is limited to the northern area of the Kruger National Park and adjoining areas to the north and northwest. A single specimen has been found along the Sabie River.

Description The various tree species in this genus differ in several respects: some have spines and others not; the fruits of some are edible, others are poisonous; five have very large fruits (up to 120 mm in diameter), the rest, including this species, have small (up to 20 mm) ones. These trees are medium-large (up to about 15 m) and single-stemmed, but the trunk invariably splits rather low down. Old stems are pale grey and fairly smooth. The bark peels off sporadically in small, longitudinal strips. **LEAVES** Simple, fairly large (mostly 110 × 50 mm) and borne in opposite pairs. Characteristic of the *Strychnos* genus, they have three (sometimes five) major veins originating from the base of the leaf. **FLOWERS** Small, pale yellow, stellate (star-shaped) and borne in the axils of new leaves (August–October). **FRUITS** Small (20 mm in diameter), spherical, green at first and purplish black when ripe. They are single-seeded, said to be extremely poisonous and take about a year to mature. The pulp is purple.

(ZIMBABWE: (Z825) GRAPE BITTERBERRY)

Centre and left: flowers
Above: fruit

Forest-fevertree (FSA632)

Anthocleista grandiflora

Boskoorsboom

Distribution & habitat This tree is found in the northern evergreen forests of the subcontinent. It occurs intermittently from the northernmost point in KwaZulu-Natal, through Swaziland, in the forests of the Sabie/Tzaneen area of Mpumalanga/Limpopo and up to the Soutpansberg. Further north, it is mostly restricted to the forests in the east of Zimbabwe and the Chimanimani area of Mozambique. Unfortunately, it will only survive in frost-free areas.

Description This very large tree is currently the only local tree species classified in the gentian family (Gentianaceae) – a family of predominantly herbaceous members.

With its enormous leaves, especially in younger plants, and beautiful, fairly large, trumpet-shaped flowers, its identification is relatively easy. **LEAVES** The Zimbabwean name for the tree, forest bigleaf, is quite fitting, as leaves may be more than 1 m long and almost 0.5 m wide. Borne close together at the ends of the branches. **FLOWERS** White, trumpet-shaped, sweetly scented and borne in terminal, candelabra-like panicles. Because the trees can reach 30 m in height, the flowers are so high up that they are, unfortunately, rarely noticed. **FRUITS** Green, oval and contain many small seeds; they develop very slowly and can be found almost throughout the year.

(ZIMBABWE: (Z837) FOREST BIGLEAF; NAMIBIA: FOREST BIGLEAF)

Notes: This is a rather slender tree with a very long, bare trunk, which is quite decorative; it should be used more often as a garden subject.

Flowers

Forest-elder (FSA634)   *Nuxia floribunda*

Bosvlier

Distribution & habitat Five tree species represent this genus in southern Africa. This one, the forest-elder, is not very abundant or dominant, but is a prominent component of the plant community, especially when in flower. It occurs roughly from George in the Western Cape to northern KwaZulu-Natal, into southern Mozambique, Swaziland and along the Drakensberg to the Soutpansberg. It is mainly associated with evergreen forest and therefore also grows in the eastern area of Zimbabwe, as well as the adjoining territory in Mozambique. An isolated population occurs in southern Zimbabwe.

Description It is evergreen and may reach a height of 15 m. Old trunks vary from fairly smooth, greyish brown and striated to flaking or very smooth and white; bark peels in papery strips. Stems are often crooked or forked and may have young shoots sprouting low down. Young twigs are purple. The crown is large, wide-spreading and dense. Trees are sometimes covered with flowers and remain noticeable for quite some time. **LEAVES** Simple and borne in whorls of three, they are fairly large, soft, elliptic, sharply pointed, pale to dark green and glossy. Margins are entire or slightly serrate in the upper half; the midrib may be reddish. **FLOWERS** Prominent, fragrant, white and, although small, are borne in masses in large, conspicuous, terminal clusters during the winter months. **FRUITS** Tiny, ovoid capsules that split into four segments at maturity.

(ZIMBABWE: (Z830) FOREST-ELDER)

Notes: The heavy, yellow wood was used by wagon builders. It is a worthwhile garden plant and can be grown from cuttings.

Flowers

Paired fruit

Paired fruit & seeds

Dehisced fruit & seeds

BRAAM VAN WYK

Toadtree (FSA644)

Tabernaemontana elegans

Paddaboom

Distribution & habitat In southern Africa, the toadtree occurs from northern KwaZulu-Natal and southern Mozambique through Swaziland, Mpumalanga, Limpopo and into southern and eastern Zimbabwe.

Description It is deciduous, but only sheds its leaves late in winter; in wet conditions it may even be semi-deciduous. It has a single, short trunk and, in spite of poor branching, the roundish crown is usually quite dense (as a result of the large leaves). Bark is soft, cork-like and splits longitudinally to form ridges that crack crosswise into oblong sections. New twigs are shiny, dark green and dotted with small, corky protuberances; they occur in opposite pairs. **LEAVES** Simple, dark green, glossy and contain latex; they are borne in decussate pairs. On young plants, they are oblong and very large (up to 230 × 80 mm, but usually about 120 × 50 mm). **FLOWERS** Sweetly scented, trumpet-shaped with five relatively long, narrow, recurved petals and borne terminally in small panicles during spring and summer. **FRUITS** Usually consist of two hemispheric mericarps, about 60 mm in length and 70 mm in breadth, which are joined to a common stalk. Their outer layer is brownish green and dotted with pale grey tuberculate warts. At maturity, fruits dehisce while on the tree to reveal the seeds, which are closely packed. Each is surrounded by a thin, bright orange, fleshy layer, which is consumed by wild animals.

(ZIMBABWE: (Z850) TOADTREE)

Top: flowers
Above: fruit

Quininetree (FSA647)

Rauvolfia caffra

Kinaboom

Distribution & habitat The quininetree favours wet conditions and is thus mostly confined to the banks of rivers or large streams and the margins of evergreen forests.

Description In drier habitats it is deciduous, while in moist habitats it is evergreen to semi-deciduous. It is one of the larger southern African trees (up to 20 m), with a single stem and a fairly dense, wide-spreading crown (26 m). New twigs always occur in groups of four at the tips of the branches, but one or more die with age. The branches and stems are yellowish grey to yellowish brown. Old bark is soft, cork-like and breaks up in small pieces. **LEAVES** Simple, oblong, sometimes lanceolate and borne in distinct verticils of five (seldom three or four). They are much larger on young plants than on old ones, turning dark green and brittle when old. The midrib is conspicuously yellow-green. **FLOWERS** Small, waxy, white, sweetly scented and borne in large, dense cymes (September–November). **FRUITS** Usually single-seeded, spherical and about 15 mm in diameter. It is initially very glossy and dark green with pale dots but, when mature, turns dark brown to black. (ZIMBABWE: (Z855) QUININETREE)

Left: stem
Above: leaves

Halfmens (FSA649)

Pachypodium namaquanum

Halfmens

Distribution & habitat It has a very limited distribution, occurring only in the very arid rock-desert region immediately south and north of the Orange River in the northwestern corner of the Northern Cape bordering southern Namibia. It very rarely survives outside this region but, in spite of this, unscrupulous smugglers have been ravaging the Richtersveld and adjoining areas over the years – even uprooting fully grown plants in order to sell them to equally unprincipled buyers, who then try unsuccessfully to establish them in their unsuitable gardens.

Description It rarely reaches 5 m in height and consists of one or more cylindrical, succulent stems with no crown. Stems occasionally branch at the base or near the apex; they are thickset at the base but taper towards the top, which is usually bent over. A multitude of spine-tipped protuberances occur on the stem. The oleander family (Apocynaceae), of which this species is a member, is well known for the very interesting plants it harbours, mostly because of the shape, size, colour and structure of either the flowers or the fruit. This particular plant's outstanding feature is its habit of growth, which inspired its descriptive Afrikaans name halfmens, meaning 'half human being'. **LEAVES** Single leaves are crowded at the top of the stem; they are simple, up to about 100 mm long, grey-green, wavy and densely velvety. **FLOWERS** Beautiful, tubular, reddish brown inside, green outside and up to 50 mm long. They occur at the tops of the stems (August). **FRUITS** Occur in twin pairs, each being fairly small, up to 40 mm long and densely covered with hairs. They dehisce, releasing the seeds, while still attached to the plant; each seed has a tuft of hair at one end.

Top left and right: flowers
Above: fruit & seeds

Poisonrope (FSA649.6)

Strophanthus speciosus

Giftou

Distribution & habitat For practical purposes, this tree is South African (it has otherwise only been found in two small localities in eastern Zimbabwe). Associated with evergreen forests, its range extends from the Eastern Cape to KwaZulu-Natal, inland through Swaziland and along the escarpment, roughly to Tzaneen in Limpopo.

Description Members of this genus are characterized by their extraordinary and remarkable flowers. Only two members of the genus may acquire tree status in our region. Although this plant usually occurs as a scrambler in thickets, it may become a small tree (up to about 4 m) when growing in the open. It then tends to form a nearly impenetrable bush with long, slender, intertwined branches. The bark is smooth and greenish. **LEAVES** Simple, pendent, narrowly elliptic, up to 100 mm long, glossy green and arranged in whorls of three; they ooze watery sap when damaged. **FLOWERS** Bell-shaped tubes of about 10 mm long, dividing into five slender corolla lobes of about 60 mm long. The overall colour is a dull yellow, but the broadened bases of the corolla lobes are reddish; they are striking. Flowering usually occurs in September–October. **FRUITS** Paired, slender, follicular mericarps, which are up to 200 mm long. They become brown at maturity and split longitudinally to release the seeds, which are crowned with a tuft of hair at one end.

(ZIMBABWE: (Z864) FOREST TAILFLOWER)

Notes: This plant, like others in its genus, is said to be poisonous and has apparently been used in the preparation of arrow poison. The roots, in powder form, are used for snakebites.

Far left: flowers
Left: flowers & fruit
Above: bark

Silver pipestem-tree (FSA666)

Vitex zeyheri

Vaalpypsteelboom

Distribution & habitat This particular species is limited to a rather small area, extending roughly from Pretoria, westerly towards Gaborone in Botswana. It favours rocky hillsides and valleys.

Description Members of the *Vitex* genus are characterized by digitately compound leaves; they often have glands in their leaves and flowers. Sepals are usually fused to form saucer-shaped structures and two-lipped, tubiform flowers. This is a smallish, upright, slender tree of about 5 m, with a fairly sparse crown. Young branchlets are covered with soft hairs. Old stems are dark grey and the bark is longitudinally fissured. **LEAVES** Consist of 3–5 leaflets, which are mostly covered with soft, silvery hairs. **FLOWERS** Generally pale mauve, seldom cream, sweetly scented and borne in terminal heads. **FRUITS** Small, roughly pear-shaped and enveloped by the enlarged, saucer-like calyx, which persists on the tree for months on end.

Notes: The common name refers to often hollow young twigs, which were previously used as stems for tobacco pipes.

Left: flowers
Above: fruit

Tree-fuchsia (FSA670)

Halleria lucida

Notsung

Distribution & habitat The tree-fuchsia is well adapted to a very wide range of climatic conditions, as evidenced by its distribution and occurrence in a variety of habitats: from evergreen forest to coastal, and even karroid, shrub.

Description It may occasionally reach a height of 12 m, but is usually encountered as a shrub, small tree, or even a climber, often with more than one trunk. The bark is greyish white to pale brown and smooth to flaking. Side-shoots and smaller, trailing branches usually occur from the base. The crown is sparse and fairly spreading with trailing branchlets. **LEAVES** Simple, 40–80 mm long, rhomboidal to ovate and borne in opposite pairs. Margins are conspicuously toothed to scalloped, but only in the upper two-thirds. **FLOWERS** Attractively curved, tubular, orange to dark red and borne almost throughout the year in axillary clusters, as well as on older branches. **FRUITS** Almost spherical to ovoid, very glossy, fleshy berries, which turn black when ripe. They are crowned by the long, thin, persistent style. The berries are edible, sweet, and relished by birds.

(ZIMBABWE: (Z914) TREE-FUCHSIA)

Notes: The wood is yellow, hard and tough, but is seldom used. This tree makes a good garden subject.

Top: flowers
Above: fruit

Yellowthorn (FSA675) *Rhigozum obovatum*

Geeldoring

Distribution & habitat This species occurs mainly in the Karoo, but extends through the northwestern parts of the Northern Cape and into the south of Namibia; it can also be found in the southern Free State and parts of the North West province. Two other species in the genus, *R. brevispinosum* and *R. zambesiacum* have a western and eastern distribution, respectively; both have spines. *R. brevispinosum* occurs in central and northern Namibia, Botswana, the Northern Cape, the North West province, western Limpopo and southwestern Zimbabwe. *R. zambesiacum* occurs from northern KwaZulu-Natal, through the lowveld of Mpumalanga and Limpopo to southern Zimbabwe and then again in the Zambezi valley. *R. virgatum,* a poorly known species, is confined to Namibia's Kaokoveld. A fifth species, *R. trichotomum*, is dominant over large areas of the Kalahari; it has white to pinkish flowers and is usually a shrub.

Description All four species have the same attractive yellow flowers. The yellowthorn is spineless, mostly multi-stemmed and may reach 3.5 m in height. Branches are rigid, as are twigs, which are also straight and may be spine-tipped. **LEAVES** Trifoliolate but often simple, as only one develops; they are very small (up to 15 × 5 mm, though mostly smaller). **FLOWERS** Fairly large (30 mm in diameter), bright yellow and very striking. They emerge only after the first good rain in spring – sometimes within days. The main flowering period is September–November; during a good season the plants are covered with flowers. **FRUITS** Brown, narrow, flattened, smooth capsules, up to 80 mm long; they dehisce longitudinally along the flat surface to release winged seeds. They are heavily browsed by game.
(ZIMBABWE: (Z918) THREE-LEAVED YELLOWTHORN; **NAMIBIA:** KAROO RHIGOZUM)

Top: fruit
Above: flowers

Bellbean (FSA677)

Markhamia zanzibarica

Klokkiesboontjie

Distribution & habitat The bellbean occurs from northern Namibia in the west, through the northern areas of Botswana and Zimbabwe to Mozambique in the east, and the warmer parts of Limpopo and Mpumalanga. This species prefers well-drained soil and is therefore usually encountered on sand or rocky hillsides.

Description It is abundant in Botswana's Chobe National Park, where some trees measure up to 12 m in height, although most only reach 6–7 m. The trunk is fairly short and often branches low down; the crown is particularly sparse and slender. The branches and stems are smooth, glossy and grey-brown to lead-grey. Very old bark is brownish grey and peels off in flat, irregular flakes.

LEAVES Very long (up to 350 mm) and imparipinnately compound, with two to four leaflets plus a terminal leaflet. They increase markedly in size from the base to the tip of the leaf. The thin, faintly glossy leaflets on some trees are hairless, while on others they are distinctly softly hairy. **FLOWERS** Bell-shaped, fairly large and beautiful. Corolla tubes can be up to 50 mm long, with spreading lobes that measure up to 50 mm in diameter. In Limpopo and Mpumalanga, crinkled corolla lobes and tubes are deep maroon on the inside and pale yellow, speckled with dark red dots on the outside. The flowers of *M. obtusifolia* are bigger and bright yellow. It has a far more limited distribution than *M. zanzibarica*, but also occurs in Chobe. **FRUITS** Fruits are unmistakable. They are very long (up to 600 mm), slender (15 mm wide), spirally twisted capsules with grey-white speckles. (ZIMBABWE: (Z922) BELLBEAN)

Top: fruit
Above: flowers

Sausagetree (FSA678)   *Kigelia africana*

Worsboom

Distribution & habitat This is a tropical savanna species, extending southwards into Mozambique, Zimbabwe, Botswana, the northern and northeastern areas of Limpopo, Mpumalanga and KwaZulu-Natal, and Swaziland.

Description This large tree can reach 18 m in height; it has an extremely thick trunk and a wide-spreading crown. Old trunks are grey-brown to dark grey and fairly smooth. The bark peels off in flat, irregular sections. It is deciduous to semi-deciduous. **LEAVES** Imparipinnately compound with two to five pairs of leaflets, borne in verticils of three near the twig terminals and can be up to 250 mm long. Leaflets are thin; margins are entire or, in young leaves, serrate. Old leaves are shed within a very short period of time and new leaves, emerging shortly thereafter, are glossy and brownish red. **FLOWERS** Large and borne in pendent, axillary racemes of up to 500 mm in length. They are roughly cup-shaped and may become as large as 140 × 140 mm. The crumpled petals and corolla tubes are deep velvety-red on the inside and red-brown with green, longitudinal ridges on the outside. **FRUITS** Unmistakable, sausage-shaped and measuring 500 × 100 mm or more; they are pale brown to grey-green, slightly rough and very heavy. The pulp is fibrous and inedible.

(ZIMBABWE: (Z925) SAUSAGETREE)

Notes: The timber is tough, pale brown and produces a smooth finish.

Top: *flowers*
Above: *fruit*

Sesamebush (FSA680)

Sesamothamnus lugardii

Sesambos

Distribution & habitat Four species of tree represent this genus in southern Africa: *S. lugardii*, *S. benguellensis*, *S. guerichii* and an undescribed species that only occurs in northwestern Namibia (Kaokoveld); *S. lugardii* occurs from the Mpumalanga lowveld (Kruger National Park) through Limpopo to the south of Zimbabwe and the east of Botswana (Tuli Block).

Description This is a small, deciduous tree, measuring 4–5 m; it has a very sparse, poorly branched crown and an abnormally thick, succulent-like trunk, which always subdivides near the ground. On older branches and trunks, bark is yellowish brown and fairly glossy; the thin, outer layer of bark peels off to expose green, living bark. Single thorns are set spirally on the twigs; initially they are soft with leaf-like appendages, but later become hard and sharp. As with all members of the sesame family (Pedaliaceae), this tree is characterized by large, beautiful, trumpet-shaped flowers. **LEAVES** Rather small and borne in groups above the thorns, even on thick branches. **FLOWERS** Consist of a particularly long, thin, red-brown corolla tube, which is elongated at the base, forming what is known as a 'spur' that extends beyond a flower's junction with the twig. The petals are crinkled and white to pale cream-coloured. Very few of these unusual flowers are produced. **FRUITS** Flat capsules of approximately 60 × 50 mm, which resemble those of the jacaranda; the flat seeds are winged. (ZIMBABWE: (Z926) SESAMEBUSH)

Notes: The timber is soft, fibrous and worthless.

Flowers

Matumi (FSA684)

Breonadia salicina

Mingerhout

Distribution & habitat This is a fairly fast-growing evergreen that occurs from northern KwaZulu-Natal through Swaziland, eastern parts of Mpumalanga and Limpopo to the western side of Mozambique and through eastern Zimbabwe up to the Zambezi River. North of that, it spreads out across tropical Africa.

Description The only specimen on which statistics have been published by the Dendrological Society of South Africa grows in Limpopo (Letaba district): height, 41 m; spread, 23.6 m; diameter of the trunk at breast height, 2.06 m. The average matumi occurring in the Mpumalanga and Limpopo lowveld has a fairly short stem, often branching near ground level, and a densely foliaged, poorly spreading crown. Old stems are grey-brown and although the bark breaks up into irregular ridges, it does not peel off. The wood is heavy, fairly hard, oily, pale to dark brown and frequently blotched. In South Africa, large trees were felled for timber at such a rate that the authorities had to intervene; it is now a protected species. **LEAVES** Simple, long and narrow (up to 250 × 40 mm), dark green, glabrous, smooth and particularly glossy, borne in verticils of four and usually set close together at the twig terminals. **FLOWERS** Minute (20 mm in diameter), pale yellow with a pink tinge and borne singly in leaf-axils in dense, spherical heads, from November–March. **FRUITS** Small and inconspicuous. (ZIMBABWE: (Z937) MATUMI)

Notes: The outstanding asset of this tree is its timber – the quality and availability of which nearly led to its demise.

Top left and right: flowers
Above: fruit

Wild-pomegranate (FSA688)

Burchellia bubalina

Wildegranaat

Distribution & habitat Found mainly in evergreen forests along the coast and mountains separating the low-lying southern and eastern coastal belt from the inland plateau of South Africa. Its range extends from near Swellendam in the Western Cape to roughly as far north as Tzaneen in Limpopo. It grows in dry forest, grassland, open woodland and even swampy terrain.

Description This is an evergreen shrub or small tree, which usually does not exceed 6 m in height. Even in the open it is upright and slender, usually with a rather crooked trunk. Bark is greyish brown and smooth. LEAVES Large, very dark green, simple and borne in opposite pairs. Transverse ridges at the nodes are characteristic and are caused by the stipules, which fall early; these are found between the leaves of a pair. FLOWERS Orange to crimson-red, tubular, up to 25 mm long and borne in dense clusters at twig terminals. Attractive and showy, they are this tree's best feature. Copious amounts of nectar, which has a strong, sweet scent, are produced. Although flowering mainly occurs in spring and summer, those in the photograph were found in Kirstenbosch during early August. FRUITS Very attractive, urn-shaped and occur in dense clusters. Leathery, horny, persistent calyx-lobes crown the fruits.

132

Left: flowers
Above: fruit

Tonga gardenia (FSA690.1)

Gardenia cornuta

Tongakatjiepiering

Distribution & habitat About seven *Gardenia* species occur in southern Africa; they are remarkable trees, endowed with beautiful, white, sweetly scented flowers. The best-known is probably *G. volkensii*, which is widespread in Limpopo, Mpumalanga, northern KwaZulu-Natal, Zimbabwe, Mozambique, Botswana and Namibia. *G. cornuta* grows in a relatively small area, occurring only in the northern part of the KwaZulu-Natal coastal region (Maputaland), though possibly also in Swaziland and southern Mozambique. **Description** It is a small, densely branched tree. The trunk and branches are pale grey, very smooth and hard; the bark flakes occasionally. It only reaches about 4–5 m in height. **LEAVES** Simple, glossy, light green, wavy and crowded near the ends of the short, stiff, nearly spinescent branchlets; they may measure up to 50 × 25 mm. **FLOWERS** Beautiful, white (aging to yellow) and sweetly scented. The corolla tube can be up to 60 mm long and the spreading lobes about 30 mm long. **FRUITS** Distinctive, ovate, smooth, up to 50 mm long and bright orange-yellow. The persistent calyx lobes initially crown the apex, but later wither away. Fruits remain on the tree for an extended period.

Notes: Although the wood is fine-grained and hard – and should therefore be suitable for the manufacturing of smaller articles – sufficiently large pieces are not obtainable. It is used as firewood.

Left: flowers
Top: flowers
Above: fruit

Bushveld gardenia (FSA691)

Gardenia volkensii subsp. *volkensii*

Bosveldkatjiepiering

Distribution & habitat This is one of the most common and widespread trees in its genus, featuring in eastern Botswana through Limpopo, Mpumalanga, southern parts of Zimbabwe, southern Mozambique to northern KwaZulu-Natal and Swaziland. It is found in a wide variety of soil types, ranging from well-drained sand to poorly drained, brackish and clayey soil, as well as rocky situations.

Description This is one of the smaller tree species and seldom reaches 7–8 m. The trunk is always short, relatively thick and often fluted; its smooth bark is pale grey with a yellow tinge and flakes in small, fairly thick sections, resulting in a mottled appearance. Twigs are borne in whorls of three and are very hard and stiff. The crown spreads wide and is relatively dense. The wood is yellowish, very hard, heavy and fine-grained. **LEAVES** Spatulate (spoon-shaped) and borne in whorls of three, they are occasionally shed in winter. **FLOWERS** Beautiful, white (turning yellow with age), waxy and may be up to 100 mm in diameter. Flowering takes place between September and December, possibly later. **FRUITS** Mostly ovoid (but may be nearly spherical), grey, prominently longitudinally ribbed and covered with greyish white encrustations. They remain on the trees for an extended period and fall unopened.

(ZIMBABWE: (Z958) BUSHVELD GARDENIA)

Notes: Only a lack of large pieces prevents the wood from being widely used. This tree is an outstanding garden subject.

Top: flower
Above: flower & fruit

Scented-bells (FSA693)

Rothmannia capensis

Witklokke

Distribution & habitat This is predominantly a South African species, extending from the Western Cape, all along the coast to KwaZulu-Natal and Swaziland, to the northern provinces, along the Drakensberg into the north but also on mountains to the west, as far as Zeerust and the adjoining area in Botswana. Although this tree may reach as much as 20 m in height in forest situations, it usually does not exceed about 9 m. It occurs over a wide range of altitudes from sea level to about 1 600 m. Habitats range from evergreen forest and riverine vegetation to rocky hillsides.
Description It is a fairly slender evergreen with a single trunk, which frequently branches low down. The crown is moderately dense and only spreads in favourable habitats. Young branches are smooth and brown; bark on old stems is fairly smooth, dark grey and mottled with brown. **LEAVES** Large, leathery, glossy, dark green and borne close together at twig terminals. They are characterized by small but prominent swellings in some vein-axils. **FLOWERS** Sweetly scented, attractive and widely trumpet-shaped with creamy-white petals and reddish markings in the throat (December–January). **FRUITS** Oval, smooth, shiny and up to 70 mm long. They have prominent longitudinal grooves, as well as a circular marking at the apex; they remain on the tree for nearly a full year.

Top: flowers
Above: fruit

Bushveld scented-bells (FSA694)   *Rothmannia fischeri* subsp. *fischeri*

Bosveldwitklokke

Distribution & habitat This species extends from northern KwaZulu-Natal (subsp. *moramballae*), in a narrow belt through Mozambique, into Limpopo. It then spreads north again into Zimbabwe, where it occurs in a narrow strip parallel to Mozambique, extending about as far north as Harare, then spreads east again to the Indian Ocean.

Description It is a small (up to 8 m), very slender, evergreen with a long, bare trunk and a fairly dense crown. On older branches, the bark is distinctly reddish brown. The colour is retained on old stems, but is only revealed when the outer layer of dead bark peels off in small, flat strips. It frequents rocky, well-drained habitats. **LEAVES** Fairly large, glossy, dark green, up to 90 mm in length and borne in opposite pairs. Small pockets occur in the axils of the veins on the undersurface of the middle section of the leaf. **FLOWERS** Showy, funnel-shaped, terminal and solitary. The funnel terminates in five tapering petals arranged in a star-pattern. The exterior of the tube is pale green, the interior of the tube is greenish white with red speckles and the petals are white with red speckles. **FRUITS** Oval, shiny, dark green with white dots and up to 75 mm long. They have a conspicuous grey, circular mark at the apex.

(ZIMBABWE: (Z959) WOODLAND SCENTED-BELLS)

Flowers

Fruit

Flametree (FSA701)

Alberta magna

Breekhout

Distribution & habitat The flametree is a beautiful, exotic-looking species that is endemic to southern Africa. This indigenous tree is found in the ravines and at the margins of evergreen forests in Pondoland and KwaZulu-Natal.

Description Although encountered most often as a large shrub, this medium-sized evergreen tree may reach a height of more than 10 m. It is multi-stemmed or low-branching, with a dense and fairly wide-spreading crown. Bark on young trunks is greyish brown and fairly smooth with transverse grooves; it becomes rough with age. A cultivated tree growing in Jonkershoek in the Cape was noted to be bearing both fruit and flowers. **LEAVES** Elliptic, dark green, glossy above and paler green underneath; they are borne in opposite pairs. The midrib and secondary veins are yellowish and conspicuous, particularly on the underside. **FLOWERS** Dramatically striking, tubular and dark red to crimson and borne in dense axillary or terminal heads. Flowering time is from January–April, but may be as late as August. **FRUITS** Ovate, small (5 mm long), but particularly conspicuous on account of two brilliant red, membranous wings attached to the apex (February–August).

Notes: This spectacular tree is a must for gardens near the coast, though it is usually slow growing and would probably only thrive in warm and humid conditions. It can be grown from cuttings.

Flowers

Fruit

Ripe fruit

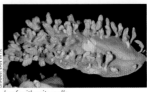

Leaf with mite galls

Wild-medlar (FSA702)

Vangueria infausta subsp. *infausta*

Wildemispel

Distribution & habitat Of the approximate twelve wild-medlar species occurring in southern Africa, this one is by far the most widespread and common, extending from the Eastern Cape northwards in a horse-shoe pattern into Mozambique and the northern parts of South Africa, nearly blanketing the latter. It also occupies most of Zimbabwe, the east and northeast of Botswana and the major part of northern Namibia. It seems to prefer a well-drained substrate, such as sandy soil, and often grows on rocky hillsides.

Description It is a small (6 m), deciduous tree with a short trunk and a dense, spreading crown; branches usually hang low on the ground. Branches and stems have pale grey-brown bark, sometimes with a yellow tinge. The thin outer layer of bark peels off in flat, untidy strips. **LEAVES** Simple and borne in opposite pairs, set fairly far apart. They are quite large, usually measuring about 110 × 60 mm (but are sometimes twice as large), very soft and slightly pubescent. **FLOWERS** Small, yellow-green and borne in dense racemes in leaf-axils or immediately above scars left by fallen leaves. Conspicuous hairs can be seen in the corolla tube. **FRUITS** Almost round. Young fruits are dark green, glossy and hard; when ripe, they are faintly glossy, soft and pale brown. A conspicuous mark at their apex indicates the former location of the calyx, which has fallen off. Two to five hard seeds are embedded in the soft, crumbly fruit pulp. Fruits are edible and quite palatable.

(ZIMBABWE: (Z987) WILD-MEDLAR)

Left: flowers
Above: flowers & fruit

Bush tickberry (FSA736.1) — *Chrysanthemoides monilifera*

Bietou

Distribution & habitat It is found over a large area of South Africa, occurring in a broad belt from roughly Springbok in Namaqualand, following the coastline around the Cape to northern KwaZulu-Natal and along the escarpment to the Soutpansberg. Unlike the vast majority of other tree species, it can tolerate even the very low temperatures prevailing in Lesotho and the eastern Free State during winter. Its abundance on coastal dunes, often near the high-tide mark, further emphasizes its remarkable adaptability.

Description Although this plant is very seldom seen in its true tree form (about 6 m in height), its sheer beauty when in flower, which occurs in winter, merits its inclusion in this guide. It is evergreen and is usually encountered as a very dense, multi-stemmed, large shrub with a roundish crown. Its bark is fairly smooth and grey. Bush tickberry belongs to the daisy family (Asteraceae) and its flowers are daisy-like in appearance, as can be seen in the picture. **LEAVES** They are simple, borne alternately, rather large (up to 70 mm) and covered with a dense, white layer of hairs when young, but become glossy with age. Leaf margins are conspicuously toothed in the upper half to one-third only. **FLOWERS** Bright yellow, fairly large (40 mm in diameter) and borne at the ends of the branches, either solitarily or in small groups (May–October). **FRUITS** The specific name, which means 'bearing a necklace', aptly describes the fruits and their configuration: almost spherical, about 8 mm in diameter, glossy, fleshy and arranged in close proximity around the edge of the receptacle. They become purple at maturity.

(ZIMBABWE: (Z1074) BUSH TICKBERRY)

Glossary

alternate (of a leaf or flower) – arranged singly at different heights on either side of the stem
aril – the outer covering of some seeds, often brightly coloured
axil – angle between the petiole of a leaf and a twig
bipinnate – having leaflets growing in pairs on paired stems
conduplicate – one half of a leaf folded lengthwise and upwards upon the other
corolla – petals of a flower
cyme – an often flat-topped inflorescence that blooms from the centre outwards, and whose main axis always ends in a flower
deciduous – shedding leaves once a year
decussate – succeeding pairs of leaves crossing at right angles
dehiscent – splitting open to release seeds
drupe – one-celled fruit with one or two seeds, e.g. a plum
edaphic – relating to the physical and chemical properties of soil
elliptic – oval-shaped
entire – with a continuous, unimpaired leaf margin
floret – a component flower of a composite flowerhead
follicle – single-chambered fruit that splits only along one seam to release its seeds
genus (genera) – group of closely related species
glabrous – with an even, smooth surface; hairless
heartwood – usually darker, harder, central part of a trunk
imparipinnate (of a pinnate leaf) – having an odd terminal leaflet
indehiscent (of a fruit) – not splitting to release the seeds
inflorescence – flowers on a common stalk
lanceolate – lance-shaped
latex – the fluid (often sticky) found in some plants
mericarp – a fruit that develops from one of the carpels of the ovary
midrib – large, central vein in a leaf
oblanceolate – inversely lanceolate
obovate – inversely egg-shaped
orbicular – round or shield-shaped
ovate – egg-shaped
palmate – of four or more leaves arising from a common stalk
panicle – tuft or bunch of flowers, close or scattered
paripinnate (of a pinnate leaf) – without a terminal leaflet
peduncle – stem or stalk supporting inflorescence or fruit
pendent – hanging down
pergamentaceous – parchment-like
pericarp – the part of a fruit enclosing the seed
pinna – primary division of a pinnate leaf (leaflet)
pinnate (of a compound leaf) – divided in a feathery manner
pubescent – covered with soft hairs or down
raceme – inflorescence in which the flowers are borne along the main stem, with the oldest flowers at the base, e.g. hyacinth
rachis – stalk or axis of a compound leaf bearing the pinnae
recurved – rolled or bent backwards
sapwood – outer layer of wood between the bark and the heartwood
savanna – subtropical or tropical grassland with scattered trees and shrubs
serrate (of a leaf margin) – notched like the teeth of a saw
sessile (of a leaf or flower) – sitting directly on a base without a supporting stalk, petiole, etc
spathe – a large bract enclosing the inflorescence
spicate – having, or arranged in, spikes

spike – inflorescence with sessile flowers along a central axis
spinescent – spiny, having sharply pointed thorns
stipules – small, leaf-like appendages that occur in pairs at the junction of the leafstalks with a twig, mostly falling early
terminal – situated at the tip
tomentose – covered with matted hairs
trifoliolate – having three leaflets
trilocular – having three chambers or cavities
tuberculate – covered with tubercles (protuberances)
tubiform – tube-shaped
umbel – flowers forming a cluster from a common centre
verticil – a circular arrangement of leaves around a stem
whorl – of three or more leaves arising in a circle at the same point on a twig

Flower

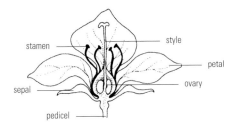

Compound leaf

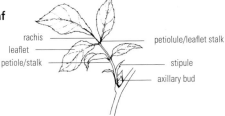

Simple leaf

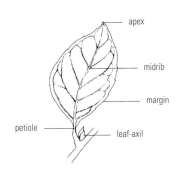

Index

144